DATE DUE

HAIR and FIBERS

FORENSIC EVIDENCE

HAIR and FIBERS

JOHN D. WRIGHT

SERIES CONSULTANT: RONALD L. SINGER, M.S.
PRESIDENT, INTERNATIONAL ASSOCIATION OF FORENSIC SCIENCES

Sharpe Focus

an imprint of M.E. Sharpe, Inc.

First edition for the United States, its territories and dependencies,
Canada, Mexico, and Australia, published in 2008 by M.E. Sharpe, Inc.

Sharpe Focus
An imprint of M.E. Sharpe, Inc.
80 Business Park Drive
Armonk, NY 10504

www.mesharpe.com

ISBN: 978-0-7656-8116-4

Library of Congress Cataloging-in-Publication Data

Wright, John D., 1938-
  Hair and fibers / John D. Wright.
     p. cm. -- (Forensic evidence)
  Includes bibliographical references and index.
  ISBN 978-0-7656-8116-4 (hardcover : alk. paper)
  1. Criminal investigation. 2. Hair--Analysis. 3. Fibers--Analysis. 4.
Evidence, Criminal. 5. Forensic sciences. I. Title.

HV8077.5.H34W75 2008
363.25'62--dc22

                                    2007006752

Editorial and design by Amber Books Ltd
Project Editor: Michael Spilling
Copy Editor: Brian Burns
Picture Research: Kate Green
Design: Richard Mason

Cover Design: Jesse Sanchez, M.E. Sharpe, Inc.

Printed in Malaysia

9 8 7 6 5 4 3 2 1

Contents

Introduction

As we approach the end of the first decade of the twenty-first century, interest in the forensic sciences continues to grow. The continued popularity of television shows such as *CSI*, *Crossing Jordan*, *Bones*, and the like has stimulated such an interest in forensic science among middle and high-school students that many schools now offer "forensic science" as a subject choice alongside the more traditional subjects of biology, chemistry, and physics. Each year, the number of colleges and universities offering majors in forensic science at both undergraduate and graduate level has increased, and more and more graduates are entering the job market looking for positions in the forensic science industry. The various disciplines that comprise forensic science provide the opportunity to use education and training in ways that the average student may imagine is rarely possible. On a day-to-day basis, the forensic scientist is called upon to apply the laws of science to the solution of problems that may link a particular individual to a particular crime scene or incident. Alternatively, the same tools and techniques may exonerate an innocent person who has been wrongly accused of committing a crime.

The four books that make up this series—*DNA and Body Evidence*, *Fingerprints and Impressions*, *Fire and Explosives*, and *Hair and Fibers*—are designed to introduce the reader to the various disciplines that comprise the forensic sciences. Each is devoted to a particular specialty, describing in depth the actual day-to-day activities of the expert. The volumes also describe the science behind those activities, and the education and training required to perform those duties successfully. Every aspect of forensic science and forensic investigation is covered, including DNA fingerprinting, crime scene investigation and procedure, detecting trace evidence, fingerprint analysis, shoe and boot prints, fabric prints, ear prints, blood sampling, arson investigation, explosives

A human hair magnified many times under a microscope. Among other things, testing hair from a crime scene can offer DNA evidence as well as reveal the racial background of the hair's owner.

analysis, laboratory testing, and the use of forensic evidence in the courtroom, to cover just a brief sample of what the four volumes of *Forensic Evidence* have to offer. Pull-out feature boxes focus on important aspects of forensic equipment, procedures, key facts, and important cases studies.

Numerous criminal cases are described to demonstrate the uses and limits of forensic investigation, including such famous and landmark cases as the O.J. Simpson trial; cases of mistaken identity, such as Will West, who was at first confused with his identical twin and eventually cleared via fingerprint analysis; notorious serial killer Jack Unterweger, who was eventually convicted using DNA analysis from a single hair; and the work of the Innocence Project, which has used DNA analysis to retrospectively overturn wrongful convictions.

In *Hair and Fibers*, the author describes the uses of hair and fibers in forensic investigation, how hair and fibers are collected and analyzed, criminal cases involving hair, and famous cases involving fiber analysis, such as that of Dr. Jeffrey MacDonald, which is still unresolved more than thirty years after the crime. Written in a plain, accessible style, the series is aimed squarely at the general reader with an interest in forensic science and crime scene analysis, and does not assume previous knowledge of the subject. All technical language is either explained in the text, or covered in an easy-to-reference glossary on pages 92–93. Taken as a whole, the *Forensic Evidence* series serves as a comprehensive resource in a highly readable format.

Ronald L. Singer, M.S.
President, International Association of Forensic Sciences

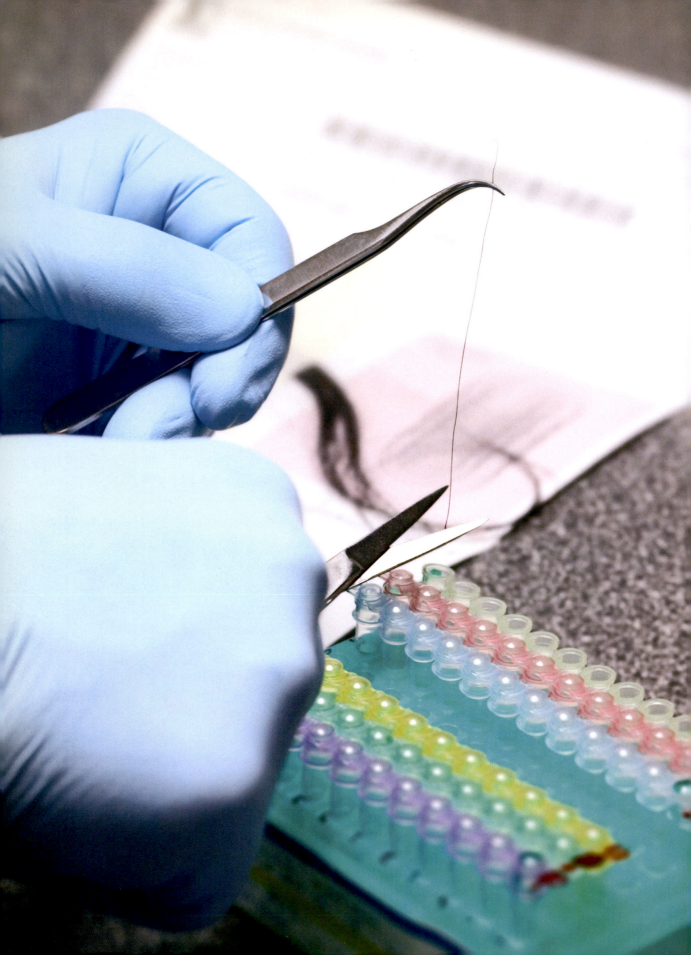

chapter 1

What Hair and Fibers Reveal

The most common clues at a crime scene are hair and fibers. Examined by forensic scientists, these clues can prove guilt.

When a crime is committed, even a careful criminal tends to leave clues, especially when violence is involved. Placing a suspect at the scene of a crime is a key element in criminal investigation. Among these traces of evidence are blood, flakes of skin, fingerprints, footprints, car tracks, mud, dust, paint flecks, firearm residue, and plant fragments. The most frequently found and analyzed, however, are hairs and fibers. Those from the criminal are found at the crime scene, and those from the victim are taken away, unwittingly, by the guilty, which is why a suspect's home and possessions must be carefully searched.

Hairs and fibers are most frequently found in cases of **homicide**, aggravated assaults, and sexual assaults, because these types of crimes normally involve a struggle or other personal contact of some sort. Other cases include burglary—for example, when a burglar's shoes pick up carpet fibers, or

◁ **A sample of hair is carefully prepared for analysis in a forensic science laboratory. Special care is taken to avoid contamination.**

A magnified section of hair shows its distinct scales and characteristics. Different racial groups can be identified through hair analysis.

the burglar leaves behind hair or clothing fibers when squeezing through a window or other opening. In hit-and-run incidents, forceful contact with an automobile leaves behind the victim's hair and clothing fibers, or even a fabric impression, on parts of the vehicle such as the bumper or windshield.

The French forensic scientist Edmond Locard devised the idea that "every contact leaves a trace" in 1920, and this became known as the "Locard Exchange Principle." Earlier, he also established the world's first crime laboratory, in Lyon, France, in 1910. Two years later, he solved a difficult murder case of a woman who had been strangled. The woman's boyfriend, Emile Gourbin, a bank clerk, seemed to have a perfect **alibi**, but Locard examined his fingernails and found minute scrapings of skin still containing the pink dust of the woman's face powder. The revelation prompted Gourbin to confess.

From the time of Locard's early success, the profession of forensic science has grown and spread across the world. Today, many crime labs are now famous, such as those run in the United States by the Federal Bureau of Investigation (FBI) and the Bureau of Alcohol, Tobacco, Firearms and Explosives (ATF).

Hairs and fibers can place a suspect at the scene of a crime, support witness statements, and connect different areas of the crime, such as the murder scene, a suspect's home or car, and the place where the victim was hidden or buried. Forensic scientists have an expert and finely detailed understanding of how hairs and fibers are transferred from one person to another, from person to object, and from place to place. They also know what makes a certain type of match important to an investigation.

Hair

One of the characteristics of hair is that, as with the skeleton, it lasts long after the body has decayed (unless it was destroyed by fire or acid). Hair also retains evidence of poison, such as arsenic, and even reveals when doses were administered, because of the constant rate of hair growth—about 0.5 inch (1.3 centimeters) a month.

The basic **morphology** of human hair is the same for everyone, but differences can be found by microscopic forensic examinations. These differences include the arrangement, distribution, and appearance of characteristics. Forensic scientists have done extensive research on the characteristics of hair and how it can be used in criminal cases. As far back as 1899, hair helped bring criminals to justice. Francois Goron, head of the French Sûreté, the national police force of France (similar to the FBI), was able to identify a murder victim because of the body's dyed hair, which led to the arrest of the killers. A few years earlier, hair identification was not as advanced. Goron had found hair clutched in a dead woman's hand, but examiners could not even identify it as human.

Investigators generally consider hairs from the head to be of greater importance than those from the body. Longer hairs give the forensic scientist more characteristics to compare, and a greater variation along the length increases its usefulness as evidence. The value of hair as evidence also depends on its type and condition, as well as the number of hairs recovered.

However, even a single strand of hair can lead to a conviction. When, in 1958, in Edmundston, Canada, the father of sixteen-year-old Gaetane Bouchard found her stabbed to death, he questioned her former boyfriend, John Vollman. Police found flakes of paint from Vollman's car in a parking area frequented by teenagers, as well as traces of her lipstick on a half-eaten chocolate bar in his car. The strongest evidence, however, was one hair clutched in the girl's hand.

For the first time, using a technique known as **neutron activation analysis**, investigators matched the hair to Vollman's. The hair's ratio of **sulfur radiation** to **phosphorus** (*fos-for-us*) was closer to his hair than hers. This evidence convinced the jury, and Vollman received the death sentence, later commuted to life imprisonment.

In 1990, in Telluride, Colorado, another single strand of hair helped investigators catch a murderer. When Eva Shoen was shot dead, police suspected her husband, Sam, but they had no evidence. Three years later, a man phoned police from Arizona to say his brother, Frank Marquis, was probably the murderer. Marquis had been in the town when the murder was committed but then made a 400-mile (644-kilometer) trip with a companion, who told police Marquis had tossed two bundles out of the car. After an extensive search, police found one bundle containing Marquis' clothes, including a shirt with one hair on it. Forensic scientist Joseph Snyder said it closely matched a sample from Marquis, based on structure and color. When presented with this evidence, Marquis confessed, claiming the death occurred during a bungled burglary. He received twenty-four years in prison for manslaughter.

A murder victim lies covered with a tarpaulin. It is essential that police keep crime scene areas clear for evidence collection.

KEY FACTS STRUCTURE OF HAIR

Hair grows out of the skin's follicle. The hair itself consists of three parts: the root (bulb), shaft, and tip. The root contains **DNA**, which can be extracted for testing, as well as blood factors. Under the microscope, the shapes of human hairs indicate the body part they came from: head hairs are round, beard hairs are triangular, armpit hairs are oval, eyelashes and eyebrows are tapered, and body hair is oval or triangular with curls.

The central core of a hair is the **medulla**, but, normally, the hair from a human head either has no medulla or a fragmented one, though people of East Asian origin have a continuous medulla.

An animal's medulla can have a complex structure. The **cortex** surrounding the medulla contains the pigment that determines the hair's color. The cuticle (the outside sheath) has overlapping scales. By examining these scales, scientists can identify different types of animal hairs, such as cat hair that has been transferred from an attacker's clothes to a victim.

Varieties of Hair

Hair is valuable to criminal investigators because of its natural variety among individuals. Differences exist among racial types: Caucasian hairs have evenly distributed pigment granules; Asian hair has a wider diameter and thicker cuticle; and African hair has large pigment granules. Examiners can tell if hair has been dyed, cut, or pulled out. Hair shed naturally has undamaged, club-shaped roots, while a hair forcibly removed shows damage to the root and may have skin tissue attached. Hair can also indicate age and sex, which is valuable in identifying victims, such as those involved in accidents.

Despite this, hair is seldom used as the only indication of guilt, because a hair match is not as exact as a fingerprint match. Lawyers tend to speak of probabilities regarding a match of samples found on a victim and suspect. The chance of using hair for identification is about the same as using the ABO blood group system.

However, hair can be used to rule out particular types of suspects. For example: if a hair identified as belonging to a white person is clutched by a murder victim, that would exclude black or Asian suspects. Hair is more reliable as a carrier of deoxyribonucleic (*de-oxy-ribo-nu-kle-ic*) acid, or DNA for short, which is recovered in live cell tissue from the root. In a recent study, the FBI found that 11 percent of hairs considered to be matches by visual inspection were proven not to be matches by DNA testing.

Investigators at the forensic laboratory of the Royal Canadian Mounted Police estimate that if they positively identify a hair as being from an individual's head, the chances of it belonging to another person would be one in 4,500. Other studies have found that the chance of a hair from a victim being on a suspect accidentally would be only one chance in 800. The chance of finding a suspect's hair on the victim—also by accident—would be one in 640,000.

Nevertheless, convictions by hair identification have sometimes proven to be wrong. In Manitoba, Canada, in 2004, DNA was used to overrule the incorrect

Girls with different types of hair pose for the camera. Hair types in the Western world display almost every variety but still require microscopic analysis to find suspect-victim matches.

Crime scenes are secured before criminologists begin their careful search, as seen here in Leyton, England, where a man died after being engulfed in flames.

matching of hairs to three suspects in separate cases. In one, Kyle Unger, then age nineteen, was given a life sentence in 1992 for killing a sixteen-year-old girl. After serving thirteen-and-a-half years, he was released on bail pending another trial, after a DNA test revealed that the hair strands were not his.

Hair is, of course, useless as evidence in domestic disputes or other crimes, including murder, if the victim and suspect live together, or did so previously.

The other major use of hair as evidence is when testing for drugs. "On your head, you have about 80,000 snapshots of your past," said Robert Kronstrand of the Department of Forensic Chemistry at the National Board of Forensic Medicine in Linkoping, Sweden. "Every single hair strand is a storage facility for drugs, medications, nicotine, and even some of the alcohol you have used." The pigment **melanin** plays a special part in binding drugs to hair.

Hair can be a record of previous poisoning or past drug use. While urinalysis (testing the urine) can generally detect drugs taken in the previous two or three days, hair can detect drug use for about the previous ninety days.

Hair can also tell us about the drugs used by earlier generations. More than

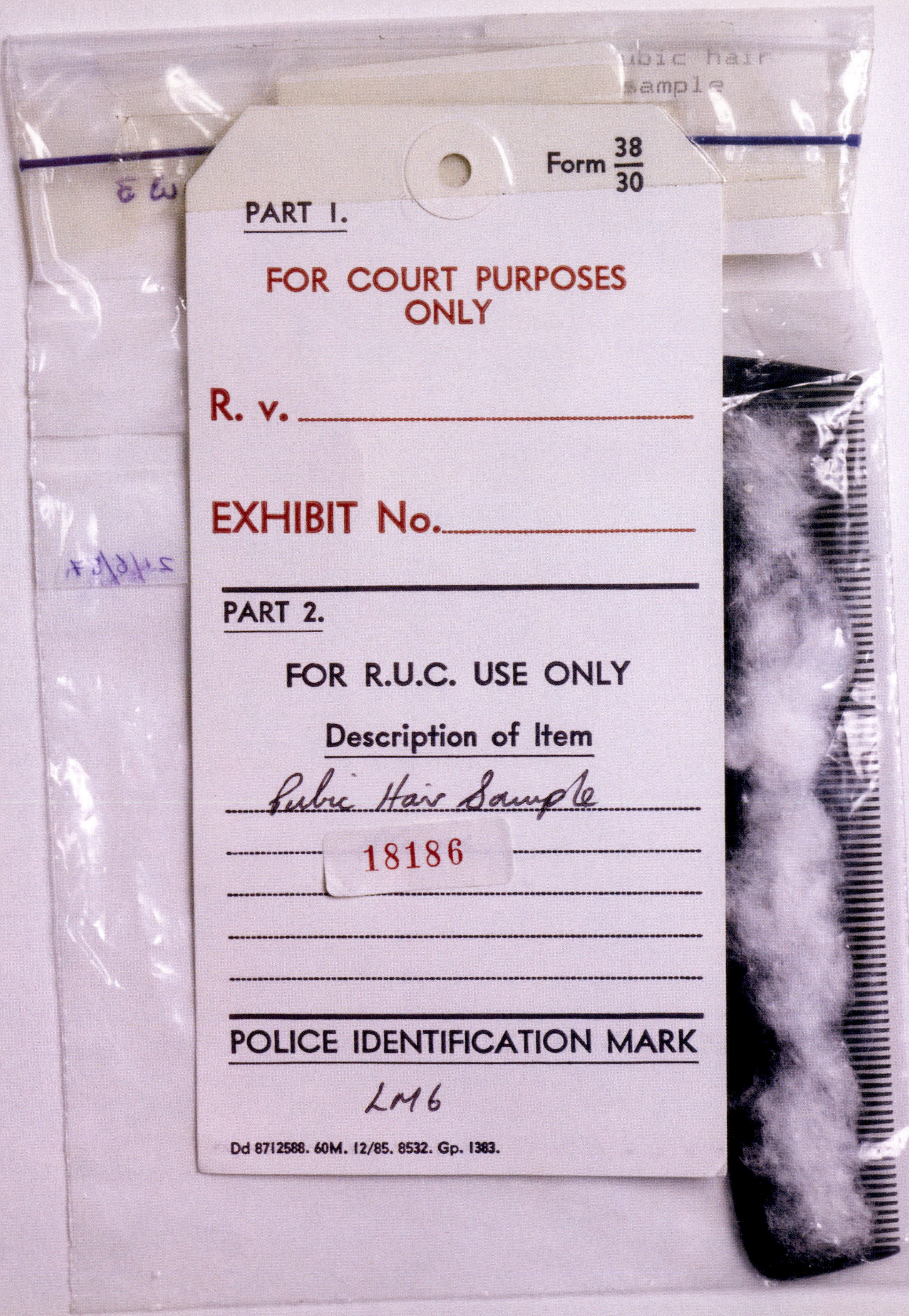

PART I.

FOR COURT PURPOSES
ONLY

R. v. _____

EXHIBIT No._____

PART 2.

FOR R.U.C. USE ONLY

Description of Item

Pubic Hair Sample

18186

POLICE IDENTIFICATION MARK

LM6

Form 38/30

Dd 8712588. 60M. 12/85. 8532. Gp. 1383.

ubic hair
sample

150 years after the death in 1821 of the English poet John Keats, a forensic analysis of his hair revealed morphine traces. It apparently came from the **laudanum** (*laud-num*) that Keats took to ease the pain of the tuberculosis which killed him.

One forensic scientist, however, has changed his mind about the absolute value of analyzing hair for evidence of drug use. Dr. Fred Smith, a professor in the Department of Justice Sciences at the University of Alabama at Birmingham, had given expert testimony in 1982 in the first court case to allow a hair test as evidence, and in several subsequent trials. Although he knew drugs could be found through such tests, his analysis of hair began to produce **false-positive** readings in the children of drug users. The hair of children between the ages of two and twelve was showing evidence of the same amount of cocaine as their parents' tests, but their urine tests came out negative. Dr. Smith soon found himself testifying for the other side. When Ten Binion, part owner of Binion's Horseshoe Casino in Las Vegas, lost his gaming license due to heroin addiction, he submitted a lock of hair, which tested positive for cocaine and marijuana. He disputed the test, saying his girlfriend used both drugs but he did not. Dr. Smith was called in to testify in Binion's defense, saying a nonuser could show evidence of drug use. (This testimony delayed the decision on whether to revoke permanently Binion's license, but in 1998 he was murdered.)

"It's difficult to admit that you could have been wrong in the past," Dr. Smith said, "but by doing that, I think I have become even more credible. The truth is, science does change. We learn new things all the time. I think people appreciate an effort to know the truth and accept it, as opposed to doggedly pursuing an opinion that can no longer be substantiated by scientific facts."

Fibers

Like hairs, fibers are often swapped between criminal and victim. Fibers are divided into two main classes: natural and artificial. The first group is made up of animal fibers, which are hairs such as wool and cashmere, and vegetable fibers, such as cotton and flax. Artificial, or synthetic, fibers include polyester

◁ **Hairs at crime scenes are collected in bags to avoid losing or contaminating possible evidence. If this procedure is not followed, a case for the prosecution could fail.**

and acrylic. A variety of fibers come from clothing, carpets, furniture, paper, and wood, and make up one of the most common forms of **trace evidence**, due to mass production of these items. Cotton is so common, in fact, that its fibers are seldom used as evidence. Such an abundance and lack of uniqueness make it more difficult to trace fibers back to a source.

The best fiber match is a physical one in which two or more pieces of fabric or cord can be reconstructed to prove that they were once a continuous piece. This is done by describing and documenting any cut, torn, or damaged edges on the items in question and connecting these to areas on known items. The best way to do this is with photography.

Among the cotton fabrics are gingham, muslin, organdy, calico, velveteen, seersucker, and crinoline. It is impossible to say with certainty that a fiber came

FBI agents carefully examine a crime scene for evidence during a field exercise at the FBI Academy in Quantico, Virginia.

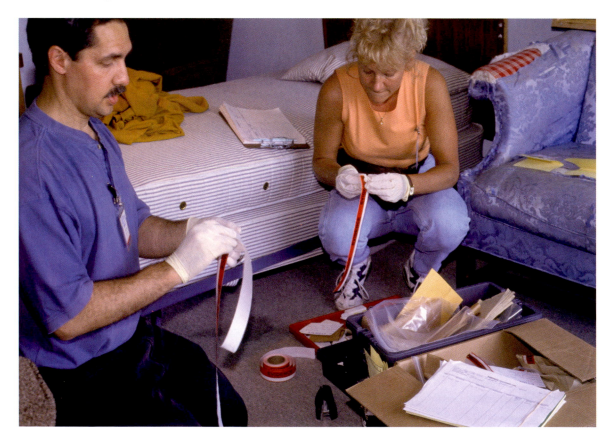

KEY FACTS TYPES OF FIBERS

Fibers are either synthetic or natural, with the latter group being made up of animal, vegetable, or mineral fibers. About half the fibers produced today are synthetic, such as polyester and nylon, which are **organic polymers** derived from **petrochemicals**, but these synthetic fibers also include glass and metal. Among the natural polymers are **acetate**, paper, rubber, and **viscose**.

Vegetable fibers are easily identifiable with a microscope and are classified by which part of the plant they come from. Those from the leaf include manila and sisal. Fruit fibers are coarse, such as coir around coconut husk, while the stem produces flax, jute, and hemp. Seed fibers include cotton and kapok.

Forensic scientists can identify a fiber by its shape, textile weave, the strand's thickness, and the direction of its twist. Cotton, for instance, is like a twisted ribbon, while linen fibers are like tubes with pointed ends. Fiber investigations also involve analyzing and comparing the dyes used.

from one particular garment, because similar garments, of the same fiber type and color, were almost certainly produced.

The most common animal fiber used in textiles is wool from sheep. The finer fibers are used in clothing, while coarser woolen fibers are found in carpets. Woolen fibers from other animals include cashmere, mohair, alpaca, and camel. When these less-common animal hairs are found at a crime scene, they have far greater significance when they link a suspect to the victim.

Still, crimes have often been solved because it has been possible to identify a type of fiber and where it was sold. In 1982, eleven-year-old Krista Lea Harrison was abducted in Marshallville, Ohio. There were no eyewitnesses and no DNA found at the scene. Her body was found, six days later and 30 miles (48 kilometers) away, with orange polyester carpet fibers in her hair. Investigators had found the same fibers eight months earlier on a twelve-year-

A British police forensic officer examines evidence, including a victim's clothing and shoes, after a terrorist bombed a bus in London on July 7, 2005.

old murder victim in the same county. Later, a woman who was abducted and managed to escape gave police a description of her attacker's van. When police found it, they noted its orange carpeting, which they traced to a manufacturer who had delivered only 74 yards (68 meters) of that particular fabric to the area. This discovery led police to Robert Buell, a former Akron city planner, who was executed in 2002 for the abduction and murder of Krista Lea Harrison.

Some fiber matches have made little impact in a courtroom—for example, during the infamous case of O. J. Simpson, who was accused of murdering his ex-wife, Nicole Brown Simpson, and her friend Ronald Goldman. An FBI forensic expert, Doug Deedrick, testified that cotton fibers found on Goldman's shirt matched those found in socks from Simpson's bedroom. He also said fibers in Simpson's Ford Bronco matched fibers on a knit cap found at the crime scene, and that cashmere fibers from the cap matched those on a glove supposedly belonging to Simpson. None of these matches deterred the jury from its verdict of innocence (*see* Chapter 3, page 42).

Forensic scientists make careful searches for fibers at a crime scene, and **pathologists** then seek traces on the victim's body. The amount of fibers they

Samples of evidence are brought to court in sealed containers. Forensic scientists sometimes argue for both the prosecution and defense regarding the importance of evidence.

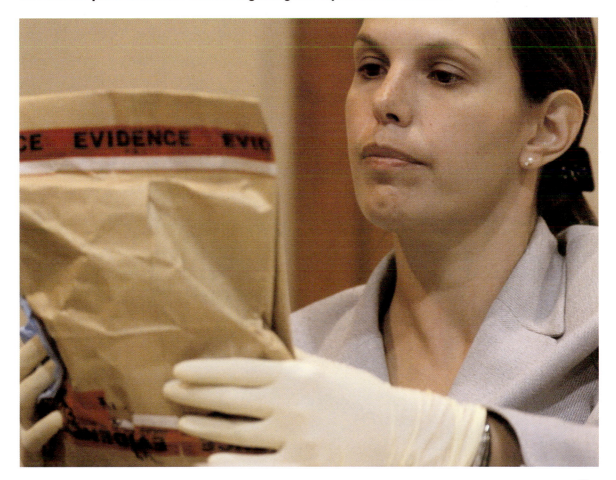

Forensic scientists are expertly trained in their specialties and make up an impressive team when working together in a laboratory.

HOW TO BECOME A SCIENTIST

Those in the forensic profession advise students to have a good science background if they want to work in the forensic sciences. The specialty areas may require different degrees. The best one for a laboratory analyst, for instance, is a chemistry degree, while someone interested in DNA testing should study biology with genetics and biochemistry. A forensic pathologist needs a medical degree.

Among the U.S. universities offering applicable programs are: the University of Alabama at Birmingham; California State University, Sacramento; George Washington University in Washington, D.C.; the University of New Haven in Connecticut; and the University of Texas Southwestern Medical Center in Dallas. Canadian programs include the University of Toronto, Laurentian University in Ontario, and Mount Royal College in Calgary, Alberta.

The renowned forensic scientist Dr. Henry C. Lee also tells potential forensic scientists to work hard and prove themselves. "You also have to learn to use deductive and inductive logic," he has said. "You need to have curiosity. You can't have an 8-to-4 attitude…. You have to have that persistence."

find depends upon the smoothness of the cloths involved. The easiest transfer occurs between smaller fibers that are less conspicuous.

If the crime was especially violent, the victim's clothing and the attacker's clothing will meet with some force and, in cases of physical assault, for a significant amount of time. Of course, investigators can make a better case if they find a substantial amount of fibers on the victim's clothing that match the suspect's clothing.

It is easier to link victim and suspect if the fibers found on both are equally worn or damaged, or have been in contact with another element, such as dust. In some cases, more than one type of fiber can be matched, as in the case of Wayne Williams, the Atlanta serial murderer (*see* Chapter 4, pages 58–60). Other cases have provided investigators with twenty or more different matches.

Fabric Color

Another good identification is color, since it is applied to fabrics in different ways. Several dyes are often used. Sometimes the individual fibers are colored before being spun into yarns, or the yarns can be dyed later before being made into fabric. Knowing how a fiber was made and colored helps with matching, as do fibers that have faded.

Fiber transfers are divided into primary (direct) and secondary (indirect) types. The former happens, for instance, when a fiber is transferred from a suspect's fabric straight onto a victim's clothing. A secondary transfer occurs when fibers—such as dog hair from the suspect's home—are transferred onto the suspect's clothing and then onto the victim's clothing. The construction and condition of fabrics affects how easily they are transferred. Loosely knit or woven fabrics shed more material than tightly woven or knitted ones. Fabrics made of spun yarns shed more than those composed of filament yarns. Newer fabrics usually shed more, but worn fabrics may have damaged areas—the result of a struggle, perhaps—that shed fibers easily.

Investigators normally collect samples from all of a suspect's clothing to compare them with fibers found at the crime scene. They must do so quickly, because transferred fibers are loose, move easily, and can drop off after a few hours. Therefore, a lack of matching fibers between the victim and suspect is no proof that contact did not occur.

chapter 2

Collecting and Analyzing Hair

Before traces of hair can be collected, a crime scene has to be secured so the evidence is not contaminated.

After a crime is committed, only a short time remains before hair evidence is contaminated or lost. For this reason, officials must secure the crime scene as quickly as possible. A forensic scientist on the scene is often called a **criminalist**. The search for evidence involves the victim and the most extensive area that might contain evidence, including entry and exit points, such as doors and windows. The general public is excluded from an even larger area to avoid any contamination and confusion.

The forensic scientist Dr. Henry C. Lee runs advanced crime scene symposiums each year for approximately 1,000 detectives from throughout the United States. He calls the crime scene "a living textbook" but believes it is often poorly read. He explained: "When you look at the history of criminal justice, not only in this country but in foreign countries as well, the problem is that in many cases the crime scene was not handled

◁ **Under the microscope, a broken human hair resembles a frayed rope. A hair's broken condition could indicate that violence has taken place.**

25

PROCEDURE   SECURING A CRIME SCENE

A forensic scientist is not the first person to arrive at a crime scene. By the time the investigator arrives, the area will be very active and crowded. The first to arrive are police officers, ambulance crews, and maybe fire crews. The forensic scientist follows soon after and finds the crime scene still virtually undisturbed because officials are careful to preserve the scene and record any evidence that they find. The area is sealed off by police tape, with one special access point for forensic investigators.

The authorities' first task is to save the life of anyone in a critical condition and to treat those less seriously injured. If suspects are present at the scene, perhaps also wounded, the police arrest and remove them. They also detain witnesses and take statements.

Before walking through the scene and examining evidence, forensic investigators talk with police to get an overview of the crime, including any information about the victim and possible suspects. The methodical search for evidence can then begin.

FBI investigators process evidence at the crime scene on October 11, 2001, after an anthrax attack at American Media, Inc., in Boca Raton, Florida.

British police collect evidence in London when two bodies were found after a storm. Any scene where deaths have ocurred must be examined thoroughly to determine the cause.

properly. We lost the window of opportunity and now the crime scene is gone. The physical evidence was not collected or was collected, but improperly. It got contaminated, or deteriorated, or distorted."

He says investigators should look for the pattern at the scene: "We have to look at a crime scene first and try to determine what's the MO (modus operandi—a criminal's usual method of operation), what's the pattern evidence, and then try to determine what happened, and when it happened. We have to determine the primary scene and secondary scene, and whether it's an active scene or passive scene, or an organized scene or disorganized scene. Once you have all of those issues resolved, you develop a hypothesis."

Crime Scene Procedure

A particular danger during a search is for investigators to deposit, by accident, hairs belonging to themselves or others, so they must use caution when examining a crime scene. For this reason, they wear protective overalls and gloves. DNA from the hands or tools of an investigator can contaminate evidence, such as the fingernail clippings of a victim or suspect. Hairs and other trace evidence should be collected before other work begins, such as removing bullets, dusting for fingerprints, and taking blood samples. The criminologist involved in the examination is normally called to testify in court about contamination at the scene.

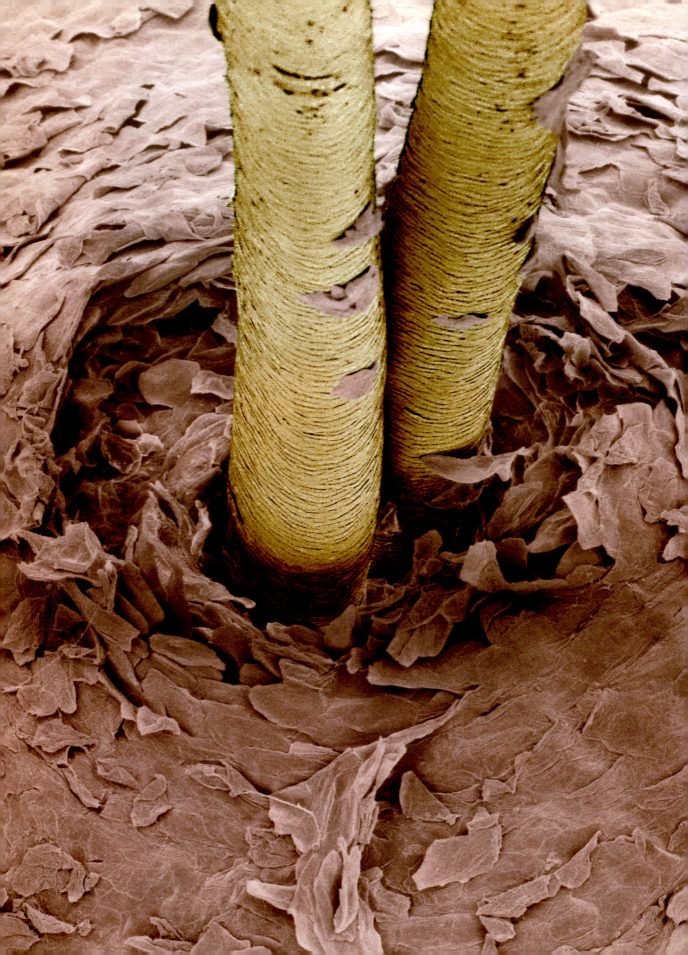

Investigators must record as much as possible—the general scene and specific details—through photography, video recording, and notes, while the scene is still undisturbed.

The most obvious way of collecting hairs is by hand or with tweezers, although the latter can damage the structure of the hair and crush the root, where the DNA is found. Investigators wear surgical gloves to avoid transferring any of their own genetic material. In Canada, the most common method is to use clear tape that lifts hair from different surfaces, even if it is not visible to the eye. Square sheets of tape can be applied to sections of a garment or object, and these sheets are labeled to identify each section. Another collection tool is a special vacuum with a replaceable filter that can be labeled to indicate the area where the hairs were collected. Hairs are often recovered from furniture such as

PROCEDURE **HOW DNA IS EXTRACTED**

DNA (*see* Chapter 1, page 14) provides the forensic scientist with the most accurate tool for matching identities—for example, when a hair on a murder victim is compared to a sample from a suspect. Investigators require only one hair from each, but it must have the bulb, which contains the DNA.

A laboratory technician will use chemicals, usually a mixture of **chloroform** (*klor-o-form*) and **phenol** (*fee-nol*), to separate the DNA from other material in the cell **nucleus** (*nu-klee-us*). Then, portions of the DNA will be selectively multiplied using a technique known as **polymerase chain reaction (PCR)**. This technique increases the sample by millions of times, making it easier for the scientist to see the DNA and work with it. The samples, which are called micro-satellites, differ in length from one person to another, and are the basis of genetic fingerprinting—the technique of identifying individuals from their DNA.

◁ **The magnification of human hair reveals, among other information, its diameter, the type of medulla, and the distribution of pigment granules.**

A police forensics team searches a crime scene for trace evidence. Searching a crime scene can be painstaking and tiring work, but a single discovery can lead to the identity of the criminal.

couches, chairs, and beds. If a vacuum has no filter, the debris is placed on a white sheet of paper, which is then folded over and taped shut.

Sometimes, investigators recover hairs by simply shaking or brushing clothes or other textile items over a white sheet of paper. The hairs and other trace evidence are then separated for analysis. To avoid losing evidence, cloth objects are often put into a bag to be shaken or brushed. Combing is the usual method of obtaining samples from a victim or suspect.

Hair Growth

Hair grows in three phases. During the **anagen phase**, the hair is growing, with active and dividing cells forming the medulla, cortex, **cuticle**, and root sheath. When a hair is pulled out in this first stage, which can last up to six years, it will have a rich source of DNA. The next phase is the **catagen phase**, a transition period lasting several weeks when the hair root becomes elongated. Last comes the **telogen phase**, a resting time in which hairs are routinely shed and can easily serve as evidence. During this phase, which lasts up to six months, a person sheds about 100 head hairs every day. The average period of growth for scalp hair is approximately 1,000 days, with a resting phase of about 100 days. Since 10 percent of the hairs are therefore resting, only a minimum amount of force, such as combing, is needed to dislodge them.

Strangely enough, hairs found in a victim's hands usually belong to the victim. In violent crimes, investigators should always take random samples of head and body hairs of both victim and suspect. The Federal Bureau of Investigation (FBI) considers twenty-five full-length hairs, pulled and combed from these two areas, to be an adequate sample of an individual's hair characteristics.

If a victim has been in an automobile, hairs may be recovered from such areas as the headrest, headliner fabric covering the inside of the roof, seats, carpet, and floor mats. The victim's socks may also pick up the suspect's hairs from the vehicle's interior.

PROCEDURE **MATCHING DNA**

Once a forensic laboratory has adequate samples of DNA from a victim and a suspect, it can produce an accurate match or mismatch. DNA analysis can even help to solve crimes committed many years ago by comparing a victim's DNA recorded on a database with that of a suspect.

Each DNA fragment is tagged with a fluorescent dye, according to its length. A DNA scanner then reads the sequence with a photo detector and displays the results as colored peaks on a graph on a computer screen. The crime scene DNA is displayed next to the suspect's sample for comparison. If the profile of peaks is the same, it proves that the suspect was at the crime scene, suggesting—with a high degree of likelihood—that the suspect is guilty.

If few of the peaks coincide, the crime-scene DNA is not a match with the suspect's DNA and therefore does not connect the suspect to the crime scene.

The Case of Ruth Hildebrand

In 1943, the body of a young girl was discovered in Oregon's Willamette River. She had drowned, but had a bruise on her forehead and signs of attempted sexual assault. Dr. Joseph Beeman, head of the Oregon State Crime Laboratory, took a sample of the unidentified girl's chestnut hair. She turned out to be Ruth Hildebrand, whom a witness had seen accepting a car ride after missing her bus. Ruth's mother insisted that her daughter never accepted rides from strangers.

The break in the case came when Richard Layton, the former police chief of Sweet Home, was arrested for a sexual assault on another woman who had accepted a lift. The investigating team correctly guessed that Ruth had also felt safe riding with a policeman. Layton's car was towed to the laboratory—it turned out to be stolen—and Dr. Beeman carefully went over its interior with a small vacuum cleaner. It sucked up a chestnut-colored hair that perfectly matched the one from Hildebrand's head that Beeman had kept. Layton was found guilty and died in the gas chamber in 1944.

Collecting Samples

When sample hairs are collected from the victim or suspect, the roots, which contains DNA and other information, should be retained. Suspects may resist having an investigator pull out their hair, but will usually do it themselves when asked. Loose head hair will come out easily if briskly backcombed; the comb should be new and not used again. The hairs are caught on a piece of paper that is folded shut and, along with the comb, placed in an envelope. A good sample is about twenty hairs each from the left and right temples, crown, and the base of the neck. The investigator should make notes of the person's age, the color of the hair, and any signs of hair treatment.

If animal hairs are needed as evidence, fifty to 100 hairs is a good sample. Once again, they should be pulled out to retain the roots. Investigators need samples of both the coarse and fine hair, which should include all the main colors. The hair should come from the head, back, underbelly, and tail.

When the hairs have been collected, care must be taken when packaging them for the forensic laboratory. Items of clothing should be put in separate paper bags, which are then sealed. Plastic bags are not used. If clothing is recovered from both the victim and suspect, these items should be quickly separated and kept in different areas for packaging. Since hairs on clothing might move or be lost, they should be removed, their source written down, and then the hairs placed in an envelope. The FBI seals them in a clean piece of paper or in an envelope, which is then placed in another envelope that is taped shut. All evidence containers are labeled with information such as the investigator's initials, the case number, source, and date.

Laboratory Testing

Hair evidence is sometimes held in doubt because of the way it is handled on its journey from the crime scene to the laboratory, a procedure called the chain of custody. In 1997, in a case of an assault on a child, Randall Scott was convicted after an FBI agent performed

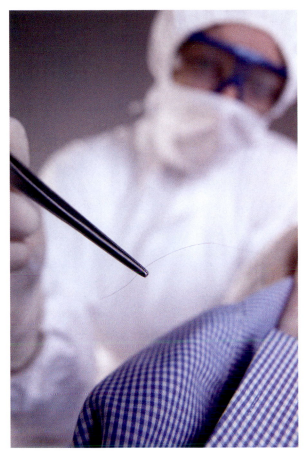

A forensic scientist examines a single hair. Tweezers are used to handle such evidence, so that an investigator's DNA is not left on the sample.

mitochondrial DNA (mtDNA) analysis on the hairs of Scott and the victim. The court concluded, however, that the state had failed to establish a chain of custody for the hairs: although the hairs had been mounted on slides for testing, agents could not prove that they were the same hairs taken from the victim and delivered to the FBI.

When FBI agents collect hairs, they send them to its Trace Evidence Unit, part of the FBI laboratory, where they are assigned to an examiner. Along with the evidence, the examiner receives information on the type of offense, the names of the victim and suspect, and the examinations being requested. The facts about

KEY FACTS BECOMING A LAB TECHNICIAN

A forensic laboratory technician performs forensic analysis tests. Salaries can range from about $30,000 to more than $40,000. Employment is available from the federal, state, and local governments, police departments, medical examiners' offices, hospitals, coroners' offices, and other forensic laboratories.

Among other duties, the technician assists professional staff in examining crime scenes and collecting physical evidence, prepares chemical solutions and performs routine chemical analysis on samples and specimens, prepares reports of test results, and testifies in court about the tests and procedures followed.

For this, laboratory technicians must have knowledge of basic chemistry related to laboratory work. High school courses should include biology, chemistry, and algebra. Minimum qualifications normally require studies of chemistry and related courses at college level. Ivy Tech Community College in Lafayette, Indiana, for example, offers such a program. Courses include: organic chemistry, criminology, criminal justice systems, crime methods and techniques, and computer fundamentals for technology. If this type of concentration is not offered, those interested in a forensic laboratory career can take related college programs, such as biotechnology.

A technician handles equipment at a forensics lab in New York City. The profession involves work ranging from the crime scene to the courtroom.

who was involved in the crime are important, because hairs from family members of those involved might be discounted in some cases.

If the forensic laboratory receives clothing or objects, rather than hair samples, the examiner must collect the hairs in a manner similar to a crime-scene collection. The clothes of the victim and suspect are processed in separate rooms, and the hairs are removed by picking, scraping, and sometimes taping, but less often by vacuuming.

Hairs are normally examined by **light microscopy.** First, the hairs of the victim are identified and compared to those of a suspect. It is important to find out if the hairs were transferred between the two people or between a person and an object. If only one person was involved—like a burglar—hairs can help to identify that person.

Comparison Microscope

The tool used to compare hair samples is, conveniently, called a comparison microscope, which was invented in 1925 by the American forensic scientists Phillip Gravelle and Calvin Goddard. (It was used two years later to match bullet casings that upheld the convictions of the famous anarchists Nicola Sacco and Bartolomeo Vanzetti.) The comparison microscope consists of two compound light microscopes with a magnification of about 40 times to 400 times. They are connected by an optical comparison bridge that allows an examiner to compare two hairs—an unidentified hair and an identified hair—by viewing them simultaneously in a single eyepiece. Both samples are placed on glass microscope slides, with the unidentified hair under one microscope and the identified hair under the other.

Although the basic characteristics of human hairs are the same from one person to the next, the microscope reveals enough variations of arrangement, distribution, and appearance for an expert examiner to contrast hairs from different people. The examiner looks closely at color, diameter, granules, the type of medulla (*see* Chapter 1, page 13), and the way pigment granules are distributed. The forensic scientist first determines whether the hair is from a human or an animal. If the latter, it can be identified to a certain species—a German shepherd dog, say—but tests cannot identify an individual dog. Forensic laboratories have extensive reference samples to aid the comparison.

chapter 3

Criminal Cases Involving Hair

Many suspects have been convicted or acquitted by hair samples. Modern DNA examinations have also solved numerous older "cold cases"—unsolved crimes.

Since Rosella Rousseau confessed to the murder of Germaine Bichon in France, in 1910, after strands of her hair were found at the scene, cases involving hair have occurred regularly in the courts. With the advent of DNA testing, and its growing sophistication, it gets ever more difficult for criminals to escape identification.

Evidence involving hair has featured in several famous cases, including the assassination of President John F. Kennedy. A blanket that had apparently covered the telescopic sight of the rifle used by Lee Harvey Oswald, the suspected assassin, was taken to the Federal Bureau of Investigation's laboratory the day after the assassination, to be tested by Paul M. Stombaugh, an FBI specialist on hairs and fibers. Stombaugh reported to the Warren Commission, which was set up to investigate the Kennedy assassination, that several limb and body hairs found

◁ **Facing a lawyer in court is part of a forensic scientist's work. A hostile lawyer will try to criticize the laboratory findings.**

on the blanket matched samples of Oswald's limb and body hairs obtained by the Dallas police.

Flawed Procedure

It is often pointed out that microscopic comparison of hairs should never be taken as conclusive evidence of a match, especially now that DNA tests have overshadowed the microscope. Numerous convicted people have been proved innocent when DNA tests have reversed hair evidence that mistakenly connected them to a crime scene.

"Everybody should always explain that a similarity doesn't mean there's not someone else with the same hair," said Dick Bisbing, a trace-evidence expert with McCrone Associates in Chicago. Charles Linch, of the Virginia Division of Forensic Science adds: "There's not any hair examiner in the country who hasn't said a couple of hairs are microscopically similar and then on DNA it turns out they're not the same hairs. A lot of hairs are microscopically similar."

In 2000, Billy Gregory of Louisville, Kentucky, became the first convicted man to be exonerated by mitochondrial DNA (mtDNA) tests (*see* Chapter 2, page 33) on his hair. He had been convicted in 1993 of rape and attempted rape in separate crimes near his home. The victims had failed to identify him from photo lineups, and his hairs were incorrectly matched to those found on a stocking mask.

Wrongful Convictions

Unfortunately, some lawyers try to impress upon a jury the "fact" that DNA can confirm a match between two samples. In the 1999 Illinois trial of Cecil Sutherland, accused of killing ten-year-old Amy Schulz, prosecutors said forensic hair testimony was based on "fact and certainty" and the two crucial hairs "could have" come from the accused, even though they could also have come from someone else. Sutherland was found guilty and given the death sentence. Later, however, DNA tests proved him innocent and he was released from death row.

In similar circumstances, in the trial of Guy Paul Morin for killing a nine-year-old girl in 1984 in the province of Ontario, Canada, the volume and types of hair

CASE STUDY **WAS NAPOLEON POISONED?**

Modern DNA testing of hair indicates that the French Emperor Napoleon Bonaparte was involved in one of the most famous cases of poisoning. After being banished to the remote Atlantic island of St. Helena, Bonaparte died on May 5, 1821. At the time, he was said to have died from natural causes—officially, from stomach cancer.

Napoleon's valet, Louis Marchand, kept a lock of his hair for sentimental reasons. Marchand's descendants provided samples of this hair for DNA analysis, including FBI tests. The various tests found arsenic levels in the hair hundreds of times higher than normal. The doses had been administered over a period of four months.

The French-Canadian historian, Ben Weider, who first questioned the cancer story, said: "Both the FBI and Scotland Yard, confronted with the results of these tests, have said that if they came across similar results in the case of a recent victim, they would have no hesitation at all in opening a murder inquiry." No one agrees, however, on who did the deed. Suspects include his British captors and Count Charles de Montholon, who was exiled with the emperor and who knew that his wife had an affair with Napoleon.

Napoleon's banishment by the British to St. Helena began in 1815 and lasted for six years until his mysterious death.

and fiber helped convict him in 1992. The *Chicago Tribune* reported: "A hair found on the victim could have come from Morin. Three hairs found in Morin's car could have come from the victim. Fibers collected from the victim's clothing and bag could have come from Morin's car and home." After DNA tests exonerated him in 1995, a special inquiry commission concluded that jurors had been "blinded by bad science."

Another wrongful conviction happened in Chicago in 1978, when Dennis Williams, an African American, age twenty-one, was judged guilty, with four others, of abducting and shooting to death a young white couple, Lawrence Lionberg and Carol Schmal. An Illinois forensic scientist testified that three hairs found in Williams's car matched the hairs of both victims. He was convicted and sentenced to death.

When evidence was later uncovered that others had committed the crime, Williams was given a DNA test in 1996 that proved conclusively that he was innocent. After serving more than eighteen years in prison, fourteen of those on death row, he was exonerated and paid $140,000 for false imprisonment. A civil damage award later gave the four codefendants $36 million, the largest such award in history. Williams received about $12 million but died of natural causes at the age of forty-six.

The Case of Ron Williamson

DNA also saved the life of Ron Williamson, who was convicted in the 1982 murder of Debra Sue Carter, age twenty-one and a waitress at the Coachlight Club in Ada, Oklahoma. The killer had broken into her garage apartment, assaulted and strangled her, then wrote on her body with ketchup. Williamson, a former star basketball player who had been in and out of mental institutions, was arrested with his friend, Dennis Fritz, a high-school science teacher. Forensic scientists made a microscopic examination of seventeen hairs found at the crime scene, and declared that they matched those of Williamson, Fritz, and the victim. The two men were convicted, with Williamson sentenced to death, and Fritz given a life sentence.

Five days before the date set for his execution, Williamson was given a stay of execution and granted a new trial because another man, also mentally ill, had confessed to the crime. This gave Williamson's lawyer, Mark Barrett, enough

Scott Peterson was convicted in 2005 for killing his pregnant wife, whose body was discovered in the San Francisco Bay. Among other evidence, experts testified that hairs found in his boat were consistent with those on his wife's hairbrush. Peterson received the death sentence and was transported to California's San Quentin Prison.

CASE STUDY — O.J. SIMPSON

Hair presented in evidence played a part in the highly publicized criminal trial of former football star and actor O. J. Simpson, who was charged with the 1994 murder of his ex-wife, Nicole Brown Simpson, and her friend, Ronald Goldman. Hairs were found on Goldman's shirt at his home, inside a knit cap discovered at the crime scene, and inside a glove supposedly belonging to Simpson.

Doug Deedrick, FBI agent and hair and fiber expert, testified in court that the hairs inside the cap, and those found on Goldman's shirt, were consistent with those of Simpson (though Simpson claimed never to have been in Goldman's house). Deedrick also said that the hair found inside the glove was compatible with those of both Nicole Brown Simpson and Goldman.

Deedrick's latter conclusion was seriously undermined as evidence when Simpson was asked to try on the glove but struggled to get his hand into it. His lawyer, Johnnie Cochran, told the jury: "I don't think he could 'act' the size of his hands. He would be a great actor if he could 'act' his hands larger." The jury in the lengthy televised trial brought in a verdict of "not guilty."

Although he won his 1995 criminal case, Simpson was tried in 1997 in a civil case, found guilty, and ordered to pay $33.5 million to the victims' families.

time to get a DNA analysis of the evidence. The tests revealed that neither man was guilty and that the experts had failed to identify correctly any of the hairs from the crime scene. In fact, the DNA profile matched the state's main witness, Glen Gore, who had placed the two men at the club that night. Already in jail on forty-year sentences for other crimes, Gore was charged with the assault and murder. Williamson died on December 4, 2004, at the age of fifty-one.

Steven Avery

The strange case of Steven Avery, freed by DNA testing, ended in tragedy. Avery had been behind bars for seventeen years of a thirty-five-year sentence after being convicted of beating and sexually assaulting a woman in Manitowoc, Wisconsin, in 1985. When DNA testing began, one of the thirteen hairs collected at the crime scene had enough root to match its DNA to the hair of Gregory Allen, already serving a sixty-year-sentence for another sexual assault. Avery, who became the 137th U.S. convict to be freed by DNA testing, became a well-liked celebrity. On October 31, 2005, the Wisconsin legislator passed the Avery Bill to prevent any more wrongful convictions.

On the same day, however, freelance photographer Teresa Halbach went missing after going to Avery's automobile lot to take pictures of cars for sale. Her partial remains were found there, as well as her SUV, which was stained with Avery's blood. Her ignition key was found in his bedroom. Avery, who had filed a $36 million federal lawsuit for his wrongful imprisonment, was quickly returned to jail.

False Testimony

Sometimes a forensic scientist misrepresents his findings. In one case, the U.S. Justice Department's Inspector General Michael Bomwich concluded that Michael Malone, an agent in the FBI's crime laboratory, had "testified falsely." In 1997, the *Wall Street Journal* reported that local prosecutors had been notified that forensic scientists had misrepresented evidence in 3,000 cases. In one of these cases, Brett Bogle was arrested in 1991 for assaulting and killing his girlfriend's sister outside a bar near Tampa, Florida. Agent Malone testified that two hairs from the head and one from the body found on Bogle's clothing

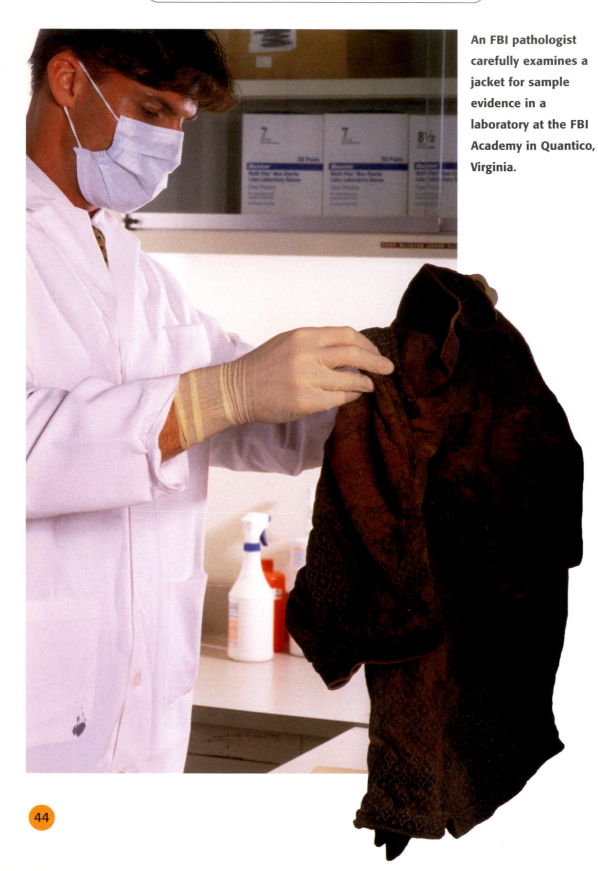

An FBI pathologist carefully examines a jacket for sample evidence in a laboratory at the FBI Academy in Quantico, Virginia.

matched those of the victim. The body hair was the strong evidence linking him to the crime. Bogle was convicted and sent to death row. After the *Wall Street Journal* investigation, however, the FBI sent Malone's analysis to an independent forensic scientist who reported, in 1999, that the body hair was actually a hair from the victim's head.

Just as important, especially to the suspect, is examiners' failure to match the hairs of suspect and victim. Hikers Lollie Winans, age twenty-six, of Maine and Julianne Williams, age twenty-four, of Vermont, were killed in 1996 near the Appalachian Trail in Virginia's Shenandoah National Park. After nearly five years of investigation, in which the FBI interviewed thousands of hikers and locals, federal prosecutors brought charges against Darrell David Rice, who was already serving eleven years in a Virginia prison for attempting to abduct a woman cycling in the same park in 1997.

Key to the case were three hairs found on clothing scattered around the campsite where the two women

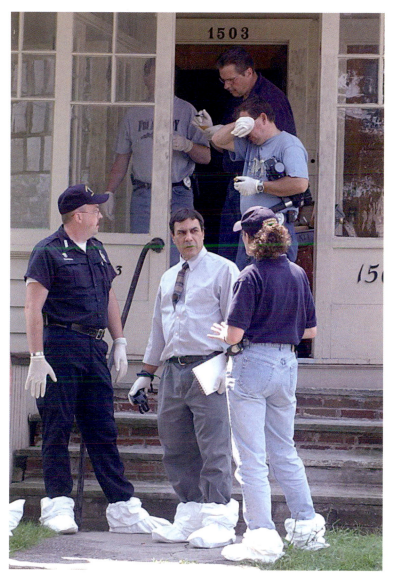

An investigator from the Medical Examiners Office in Syracuse, New York, talks with police at a murder scene. Investigating officers always cover their feet and hands to avoid contaminating evidence.

were killed. The FBI's forensic laboratory examined the hairs and said the DNA in Rice's hair did not match that of the dead hikers. Rice was exonerated in 2004, and the case remains unsolved.

Evidential hairs that fail to match will often free a suspect or overturn a false confession. In 2006, John Mark Karr confessed to killing six-year-old JonBenet Ramsey, who was murdered in 1996 in Boulder, Colorado (*see* Chapter 4, page 56). Karr was arrested in Bangkok, Thailand, and flown to Los Angeles and then to Boulder. At the Denver Police Department's crime laboratory, DNA testing of Karr's hair revealed that it did not match hair found on the blanket that had

Prosecuting attorney James A. Willett points to John Allen Muhammad during his trial in 2003 in Virginia. Trace evidence helped convict Muhammad and Lee Boyd Malvo of being the snipers who killed ten people in Washington, D.C.

covered JonBenet's body in the family basement. Karr was immediately released and sent to Sonoma County, California, to face unrelated charges for child pornography, which were later dropped because of lost evidence.

Animal Hairs

Animal hair from pets has also been used to secure convictions, as happened during the trial of Cecil Sutherland for the abduction, assault, and murder of ten-year-old Amy Schulz in Kell, Illinois, in 1987. Investigators found dog hair on the socks, shoes, underwear, shorts, and shirt the girl had been wearing before her death. More hairs were recovered from the area around the murder site. Jurors heard from a hair-analysis expert with the Illinois State Police

---

KEY FACTS | **PROBLEMS WITH DNA TESTIMONY**

DNA evidence in court is generally assumed to be irrefutable and cannot be contested. Although DNA can identify a suspect almost beyond a reasonable doubt, forensic scientists must be careful about how the evidence is presented in a court case. DNA is a virtual mystery to most jurors, and Virginia's Assistant Attorney Ronald M. Huber describes presenting DNA evidence in court as "an educational process for the jury."

It is also open to clever moves by defense attorneys, who can point out flaws in the science and try to call the evidence into question. Investigators, therefore, have to collect and handle evidence carefully. DNA evidence, for example, cannot be dropped on the laboratory floor.

The defense knows that there is no such thing as an error-free DNA database, because "false positives" can—and do—occur and wrongly identify an innocent person. Errors range from one in 100 to one in 1,000. Some DNA evidence is also difficult to interpret, especially when crime scene samples are degraded and contain more than one person's DNA. Even if DNA proves that a suspect was at the crime scene, that person might have been there at another time, and not while the crime was committed.

crime laboratory that the hairs had definitely come from Sutherland's dog, Babe. The DNA test failed to find a match to five dogs owned by the Schulz family and other dogs owned by neighbors.

Questgen Forensics conducted mtDNA testing on the hairs and compared the results to its database of 345 dogs, concluding that the DNA sequence would occur only 2.6 percent of the time. Other evidence that backed up the finding included two body hairs from Sutherland found on the girl, fibers from his clothing, and a tire track. In 2004, after spending more than a decade on death row, Sutherland was reconvicted and again sentenced to death.

Another case involving both dog and human hair involved the murder of Misty April Morse, age twenty-two, whose body washed up on the shore of Florida's Indian River lagoon in 2000, her hands and feet bound with rope, and her head wrapped in duct tape. The main suspect, on circumstantial evidence, was her boyfriend Brent Huck. Investigators found dog hair on the duct tape and the rope. After DNA testing, a forensic scientist concluded that the hairs belonged to Huck's Rottweiller/German shepherd dog, which Morse herself had given him as a gift. Hairs found in Huck's boat were also identified as belonging to Misty Morse. This combination of evidence brought in a guilty verdict with life imprisonment.

Matching Wild Animal Hairs

While the hairs of pet dogs and cats sometime feature in murder cases, the matching of wild animal hairs has occurred in environmental cases. In an unusual hoax, five federal and two state government researchers were caught planting hairs from the threatened Canadian lynx in an area of Washington state that the animal does not inhabit. According to *Environment News*, published by the Heartland Institute in Chicago, the researchers were conducting a four-year study of fifty-seven forests in sixteen sites, to see what additional steps could be taken to protect the lynx.

After allegations were made, forensic scientists from the Forest Service tested the supposedly planted hairs and found that they matched those from a lynx in

▷ **House dust magnified by 26 times reveals fiber, hair, and other debris. Without this microscopic view, possibly incriminating evidence would not be revealed.**

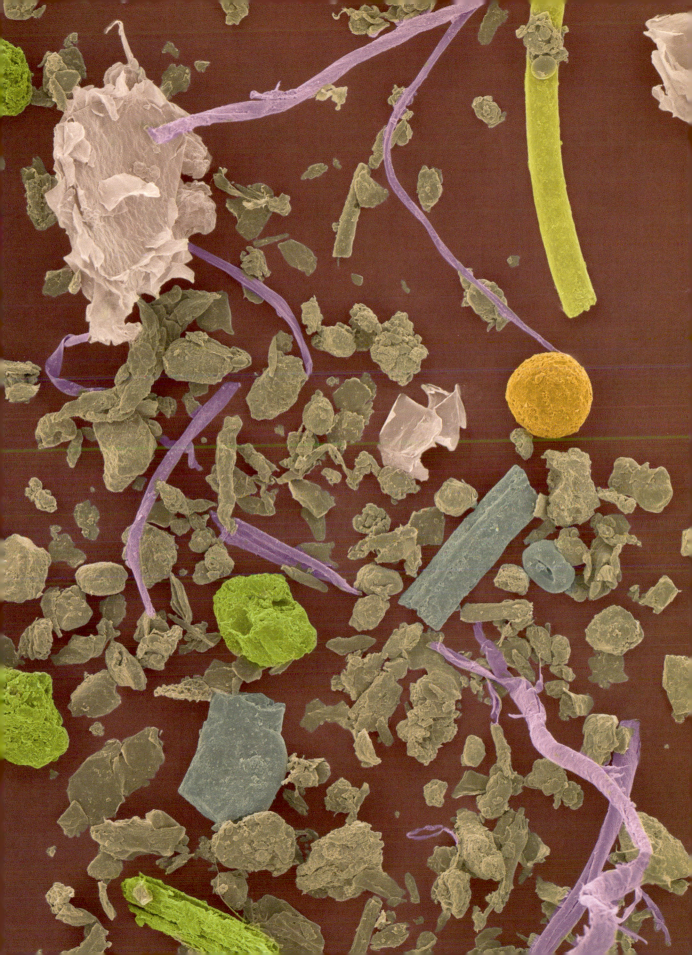

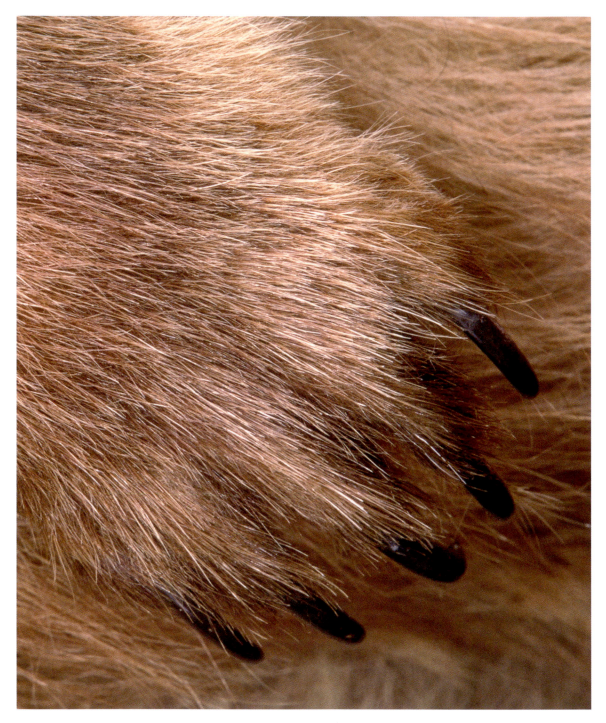

The hair of a brown bear, like other animals, can be distinguished from human hair. The cuticle, which is the outside sheath, identifies different animal types.

an animal preserve and from a pet lynx belonging to a federal employee. If the fraud had not been discovered, large-scale land restrictions affecting homeowners, loggers, skiers, and many others would have been enacted. "If they hadn't been caught," noted Senator Larry Craig from Idaho, "you might have seen entire forests shut down on a false premise."

After the lynx hoax was reported, a taxidermist in Washington state revealed that government researchers had asked for hairs from a grizzly bear rug to plant as part of a similar study involving threatened bears.

In a lighter vein, testing was done on a tuft of coarse, dark hair found by Trent Smarch of Teslin in Canada's Yukon province. Nine locals had seen, in the bush, a large mysterious animal covered in hair and believed it to be Sasquatch, the Canadian version of Bigfoot. The hair was sent to David Coltman, a wildlife geneticist at the University of Alberta. Coltman extracted the DNA, ran an mtDNA analysis, and compared the findings to a database of known animals in the region. He then called a press conference to announce that the hair perfectly matched that of a bison.

CASE STUDY **CHRISTIE WILSON**

In rare cases, forensic science can convict a killer when there is no body. In the early hours of October 5, 2005, Christie Wilson, age twenty-seven, left the Thunder Valley Casino in Lincoln, California, near Sacramento, with Mario Garcia, age fifty-three, and disappeared shortly after. Garcia went to a medical center to be treated for scratches and claw marks on his arms, as well as a black eye. He told police officers that the marks came from poison oak and that he and Christie had said goodbye in the casino parking lot.

Police, however, discovered one hair in Garcia's car, and DNA evidence proved it was Wilson's. He was charged on October 14, 2005, and convicted of her murder on November 21, 2006. Jurors said that they had been concerned because Wilson's body had not been found, but the DNA test on the hair proved that Garcia was lying.

chapter 4

Collecting and Analyzing Fibers

Fibers transfer easily between a criminal and victim. Matching them can solve a case, despite problems in tracing their origin.

Fibers, like hairs, are an important element in placing a suspect at the scene of a crime in a criminal investigation. Textile fibers from the suspect's clothing can be found at the crime scene, and those from the victim's clothing or the crime scene can be discovered on the suspect's clothing. The importance of such evidence depends upon several factors, including the type and number of fibers found; the number of different fibers found at the crime scene, or on the victim, that match the suspect's clothing; the location of the fibers at the scene; and their color or variation of color.

"When a fiber found on the clothing of a victim matches the known fibers of a suspect's clothing," said Douglas Deedrick of the Federal Bureau of Investigation (FBI), "it can be a significant event. Matching dyed synthetic fibers or dyed natural fibers can be very meaningful, whereas the matching of common fibers such as white cotton or blue denim cotton

◁ **A police photographer is vital in recording a crime scene. It is important to photograph a victim and evidence in their original positions.**

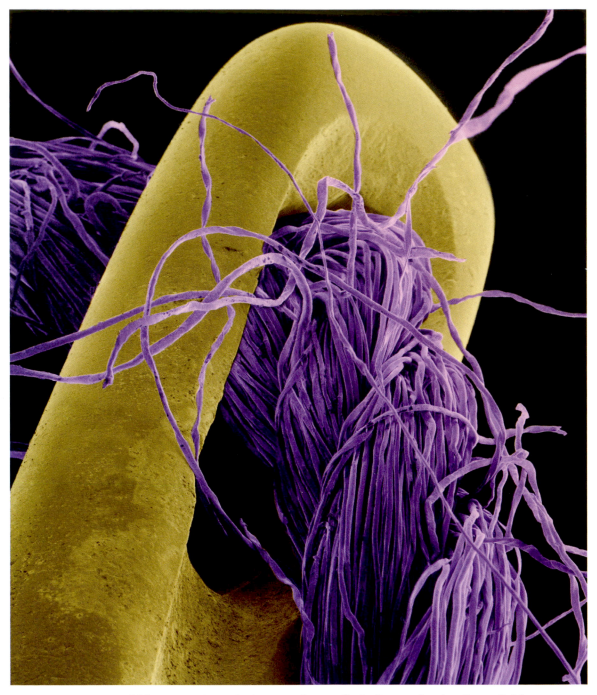

A microscopic view of fiber seen through the eye of a needle indicates the details available to forensic scientists. This greatly increases the chances of identifying and matching the immense varieties of fiber.

would be less significant. In some situations, however, the presence of white cotton on blue denim cotton may still have some meaning in resolving the truth of an issue." He added: "The discovery of cross transfers and multiple fiber transfers between the suspect's clothing and the victim's clothing dramatically increases the likelihood that these two individuals had physical contact."

Types of Fiber

Although fibers are normally transferred during contact between attacker and victim, this does not always happen. Some types of fabrics do not shed easily and others do not hold fibers well. The amount of fiber transferred, if any, will also depend on the condition of the fabric, as well as the force and duration of the contact. Incriminating fibers are often found in the pockets and seams of garments.

Investigators must not delay in collecting loose fibers and clothing from the victim and suspect. Even a day after the crime, the chance of finding transferred fibers on a suspect's clothing may be slim. They fall off easily when clothing is handled and, worse, the criminal may clean the garment or otherwise remove incriminating fibers. Little fiber loss will occur if a victim is murdered or immobilized, of course, but a moving victim can shed fibers that would be useful in evidence.

In some extraordinary cases, investigators must wait for months or years to visit a crime scene. In one case, members of the Boston Police Department crime laboratory found orange fibers with a body but had to wait two years to examine the

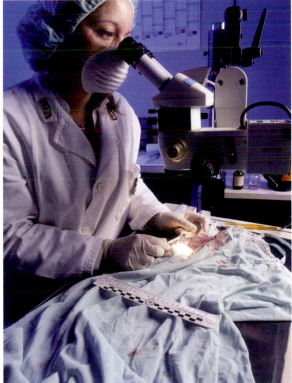

A forensic lab technician examines a large piece of material from a dress. This can identify the fiber and find any trace evidence on it.

CASE STUDY JONBENET RAMSEY

The six-year-old beauty queen JonBenet Ramsey was found murdered on December 26, 1996, in the basement of her family's house in Boulder, Colorado. The subsequent investigation has been criticized for mistakes made by the local police at the crime scene, and by the district attorney's office in their evaluation of fibers found on the girl's body.

Called to the scene, the police did not seal off the area and allowed friends to walk in and out of the house. Forensic evidence was not protected, and the police did not conduct a proper search of the house. In fact, the girl's father, John Ramsey, found her body.

Fibers found on the duct tape and rope used to bind JonBenet matched a red sweater that her mother, Patsy Ramsey, had worn the previous day. This aroused the suspicions of authorities, but forensic scientists knew that the fibers were most likely an example of secondary transfer, since her mother had tucked JonBenet into bed that night with a blanket that also had duct tape on it.

After a lengthy period of being prime suspects in their daughter's murder, the Ramseys were eventually cleared by DNA tests.

suspected crime scene. It had taken that long for the police to get a warrant to search the apartment where, according to a witness, the killing had taken place. Hopes of finding evidence were dim. There was no orange carpet to be seen, only a tiled floor. Around the base of a radiator, however, orange fibers were discovered, and these helped convict the suspect.

Fibers are collected in the same manner as hair, using tweezers, tape, or a vacuum. They are found on the victim and in virtually any part of a room, especially on carpets and furniture. A person sitting on a chair cushion may leave thousands of minute fibers there. As with other trace evidence, any findings should be photographed at the crime scene, on a white plain sheet of paper, with a ruler or measuring tape next to it to record the size. Investigators place the camera on a tripod over each item, and often use blue and green filters to enhance the appearance of the fibers. The fibers are then wrapped in clear paper, which is folded shut and sealed, or stored in a sealed envelope. Whenever possible, an entire garment or textile should be sent for examination.

Avoiding Contamination

As with hair evidence, investigators must be careful to avoid contaminating fibers discovered at the crime scene. Contamination at the scene, in transit, or in the forensic laboratory can throw a case into confusion by making the evidence useless. Such contamination might also lead to an innocent suspect being "proven" guilty, as happened in Canada, in 1986, in the trial of Guy Morin.

Morin was accused of murdering his neighbor's child, nine-year-old Christine Jessop, who disappeared from her home in 1984 and was found dead three

A textile manufacturing plant in Shanghai, China, is an example of the worldwide extent of the industry, a fact that makes it difficult to trace the origin of materials.

months later. Tens of thousands of hairs were collected in the area but investigators for the Centre of Forensic Sciences, a facility operated by the Ontario government in Toronto, contaminated the evidence. The hair evidence could not be linked with Morin, who was acquitted in 1986, though many people felt that the contamination had ruined the case. The Crown exercised its right to appeal the verdict, and Morin was convicted at his second trial in 1992. Advances in DNA testing, however, revealed that he was innocent and led to his acquittal.

Matching and Tracing Fibers

Fibers collected in a criminal case have both an advantage and disadvantage over hair. More than 100 billion pounds of fiber are produced each year. Although textiles, in terms of materials, weaves, and colors, are much more diverse than hair, so many clothes are mass-produced that it is more difficult to trace items to their original manufacturer and the stores that sold them. Manufacturing details are normally available in the garment labels. However, it is extremely difficult to find out how many fabrics with a particular fiber type and color exist, as well as who owns them. Forensic laboratories do not have access to a fiber database for comparisons.

Investigators can occasionally link a particular fiber's color and fabric type to a suspect's clothing. It is unlikely that two or more manufacturers would duplicate all aspects of a fabric type and color. A fiber link by color is significant because of the large number of dye types and colors that exist, coupled with the unlimited number of possible dye combinations.

The Case of Wayne Williams

A prime example of tracing evidence to its source occurred in the case against the Atlanta child killer, Wayne Williams. The city lived in fear from 1979 to 1981 as the death toll mounted: more than twenty-five black males, including children, were murdered by strangulation, bludgeoning, or asphyxiation. The only clues were fibers found on several of the bodies: one, violet acetate, and the other a yellow-green nylon. Dog hairs were also found on the victims.

Early one morning, during a stakeout, police officers heard something being

Microscopic examination can identify fibers by their shape and weave, such as this example of flax. Additional testing is done to determine the type of dye used.

thrown off a bridge over the Chatahoochee River. In the vicinity they discovered Williams, age twenty-three, a photographer and music promoter. They briefly questioned him in his white Chevrolet station wagon before letting him go. Two days later, the body of a man, age twenty-seven, was discovered in the river. He had one yellow-green fiber in his hair. Police immediately turned their attention back to Williams. During a search of his house, they noted a yellow-green carpet, which they turned over to Federal Bureau of Investigation's (FBI) forensic scientists. With help from the manufacturer, DuPont, they traced the fibers to a textile company in Boston that had also supplied the textile to several other companies—and each had used its own dye. One company in Georgia had chosen a dye that matched Williams' carpet.

Now the odds had to be calculated. The company estimated that only eighty-two houses in Georgia had bought carpet of that color. Inspectors also recalled that one murder victim had a single rayon fiber on his shorts that resembled the carpeting in Williams' station wagon. Assisted by Chevrolet, they calculated that there was a one in 3,828 chance of the victim coming into contact with a vehicle with this carpeting. When they added this figure to the chances of the fiber found on the victim in the Chatahoochee River also matching the carpet in Williams' home, the odds lengthened to one in nearly 30 million.

In court, the prosecution presented twenty-eight fiber types from twelve victims that could be linked to Williams. He was found guilty, given two life sentences, and the serial killings stopped.

Wayne Williams talks to police outside his home on June 9, 1981. Fibers were key evidence that led to his conviction eight months later for the Atlanta murders.

> ## KEY FACTS SYNTHETIC FIBERS
>
> Synthetic, or artificial, fibers are always made from chemicals. They are thermoplastic (softened by heating), so manufacturers can easily shape them. They tend to catch fire easily and burn rapidly. Some of the most common are:
>
> - Acetate, produced from wood fibers, also known as cellulose (*sell-u-lowse*), and woven into fabrics that look like silk.
> - Acrylic, made from petroleum and natural gas. It is lightweight and used to make soft fabrics that resemble wool. Orlon is a familiar trademark name.
> - Nylon, which comes from petroleum, was first knitted into hosiery. It is strong, versatile, and can be found in netting and carpeting.
> - Polyester, made from petroleum, coal, air, and water. Light but strong, it keeps its shape and is colorfast. When blended with cotton, it creates a permanent-press quality. Dacron is a well-known trade name.
> - Rayon, made from cellulose, can be produced to resemble natural fabrics. It has many of the qualities of cotton. It wrinkles easily but drapes well.

Matching and Coincidence

When fiber matches are found, a suspect's lawyer may try to explain this as coincidence, but this is a weak defense. "When fibers that match the clothing fibers of the suspect are found on the clothing of a victim," said Douglas Deedrick, chief of the FBI's Trace Evidence Unit, "two conclusions may be drawn: The fibers originated from the suspect, or the fibers originate from another fabric source that not only was composed of fibers of the exact type and color, but was also in a position to contribute those fibers through primary or secondary contact. The likelihood of encountering identical fibers from the environment of a homicide victim—that is, from his or her residence or friends—is extremely remote."

In the case of Wayne Williams, however, Chet Dettlinger, a former assistant to the Atlanta Chief of Police, suggested just such a remote possibility. After he and other ex-policemen independently investigated the case, Dettlinger acted as a consultant to Williams' defense lawyer and wrote *The List*, a book about the case. He noted that the matching carpet fiber found at the Williams house was also to be found at the local Walmart and K-Mart. He pointed out that Williams was living with his parents, so that they and any visitor to the home would be in contact with the carpet, which was in the living room and parents' bedroom. Four other people had been in the house regularly. Dettlinger also noted that the prosecution only considered carpets in homes, but the same fiber was found in many

An investigator's tool case at the scene of a crime will contain such essential equipment as tweezers, brushes, scissors, and a magnifying glass.

PROFILE SIR ALEC JEFFREYS

British geneticist Alec Jeffreys discovered DNA fingerprinting. The concept, that each person has a unique pattern of DNA fragments, just came to him one morning, and by the afternoon he had devised its forensic use. Born in 1950 in Oxford, England, Jeffreys graduated from the university there and then went to the University of Amsterdam from 1975 to 1977 as a research fellow. He next joined the department of genetics at the University of Leicester in England, becoming a professor of genetics there in 1987, three years after his important discovery. He was knighted in 1994. Jeffreys' current research is about genetic variability and mutation in human and animal DNA.

"Forensic DNA testing," he said, "raises concerns about the types of genetic information that police should or should not be allowed to access, and about the ways that such information should be databased and used ... Forensic DNA analysis further raises broad issues about the role of science in the court."

apartments and businesses, and had been sold, without being dyed, for car mats. He also suggested that the fibers could have come from a Laundromat where hundreds or thousands of fibers become mixed.

In the forensic lab, the fiber analyst deals with both known samples, such as a carpet section from the suspect's home, and questioned samples, which are items of evidence that have a known location but an unknown origin, such as loose fibers taken from a victim's clothes. Tests comparing the two determine whether they have the same chemical, microscopic, and optical properties. An FBI examiner, for example, has to verify at least two of three categories: generic class (the group it belongs to), physical characteristics, and color. To accomplish this, a forensic scientist first tries to match fabrics by their size, shape, dye, chemical composition, and how they appear under a microscope, which will show unusual shapes, as well as surface pits and striations (grooves or markings).

TOOLS   INSTRUMENTS AND DEVICES

There are many instruments used by forensic scientists to compare fibers:

Electron microscope—used to magnify fiber samples for analysis, typically up to 100,000 times. It reveals great differences between fibers when seen in cross-sections. Different animal fibers have their own type of scales and varied thicknesses, while synthetic fibers are different in their shape, chemical analysis, and refractive index—which measures how they bend light as it passes through them.

Comparison microscope—consists of two compound microscopes joined by an optical bridge and allows the questioned and known fibers to be positioned side by side at the same magnifications for comparison. For the questioned fiber to originate from the known textile, it either has to be the only fabric of that type ever produced or now existing—or someone must have observed the transfer of fibers. Neither is likely, so fiber examiners can say only that the questioned fiber is consistent with the known fiber if the two samples produce the same results in all tests. In placing loose fibers on the same slide when using a comparison microscope, the examiner has to take care not to confuse their sources.

Microspectrophotometer (*micro-spec-tro-fo-tometer*)—this instrument provides the best forensic analysis. It combines several instruments: a microscope, spectroscope, and photometer. It finds minute fabric traces and examines the light interacting with the fabric. If linked to a computerized spectrophotometer, the examiner can see both a magnified version and an infrared pattern.

Molecular spectroscopy and **digital imaging**—this is a promising new technology that uses chemical imaging for the forensic examination of fibers. The method intensifies a microscopic analysis of color and fluorescence in fibers, and could replace conventional microspectrophotometry.

Optical compound microscope—a series of lenses that magnify light reflected from the surface of a fiber. The microscope shows surface details and cross-sections of the fibers, and is used to identify vegetable fibers by sorting out the same type of fibers that were spun in different ways. This microscope is also helpful in identifying animal hairs.

Polarized light microscope—used to examine the birefringence (*bire-frin-gence*) of fibers, especially synthetic ones. Birefringence is the refraction of light through a material in two slightly different directions to form two rays. Light travels through the fiber differently, depending on whether it is parallel with the fiber axis or perpendicular to it. The makeup of the questioned fiber causes a different refraction that can be measured and compared to the known values of different types of fibers, such as acrylics, polyesters, and nylons.

Scanning electron microscope—similar to the electron microscope, this is used to display photographic images.

Spectrometer—separates light into its different wavelengths. When light passes through fibers, it produces a spectrum broken into absorption lines, which an examiner then reads. An infrared spectrometer measures the wavelength and intensity of the absorption of infrared light by a fiber sample. When its molecules absorb infrared radiation, they vibrate and rotate. These reactions are recorded in a spectrum that identifies the material by its type of bonds.

Forensic investigators scan clothing with ultra-violet light in search of microtraces of hair and fibers.

chapter 5

Criminal Cases Involving Fibers

Many high-profile cases have been solved by matching different types of fibers from such items as clothes, carpets, and blankets.

As early as 1912, forensic scientists in the United States were using the microscope to solve murder cases. On April 11 of that year, millionaire George Marsh, age seventy-eight, was found murdered on the highway near Lynn, Massachusetts. He had been shot to death. The single clue was an overcoat button with a piece of cloth attached. Some witnesses had seen a blue convertible car near the victim's home, and this led to a landlady who reported that she had had a guest who drove such a car. He had registered as "Willis A. Dow" and departed after the murder, leaving behind an overcoat with all the buttons removed, probably so they could not be identified.

As the Massachusetts police had no forensic laboratory at that time, they sent the button and overcoat over to the Lowell Textile School. The microscopic examination there revealed that the fragment of cloth on the button matched the overcoat's

◁ **Giving forensic evidence in court requires a technical understanding of lab procedures and the ability to explain them in language a jury can understand.**

67

texture, weave, and colors. The school's professors could even identify which button they had because of its broken threads.

Although the forensic work linked the button to Willis A. Dow, nobody knew who he was. Amazingly enough, he had thrown away the murder weapon, a .32 Colt revolver, just 50 yards (46 meters) from Marsh's body. Police traced it through its serial number to William A. Dorr in Stockton, California. An investigation revealed that he had been courting a woman who left him money in her will. Her funds, however, were tied up by her trustee, George Marsh, so

Nylon carpet fibers are seen here under the microscope. Nylon is among the synthetic types that make up about half of all fibers.

Dorr had traveled across the country to kill him. Dorr was convicted and executed in 1914 in the electric chair.

Surprisingly, the identification of cheap carpet made from leftover materials is easier to match. In 1993, in Alaska, the body of Judi Burgin, a thirty-four-year-old poet, who had various jobs, including cooking on commercial fishing ships from Kodiak, was found in the woods, wrapped in two sheets. Burgin had died from head injuries caused by a blunt instrument, and had been dead four months. The prime suspect was her boyfriend, Carl Brown, who had supplied her with drugs and, as she had revealed to friends, often intimidated her.

Within the sheets around her body, investigators found a tuft of red carpet material and a few orange and pink fibers. The Alaska State Crime Laboratory brought in Skip Palenik, president of Microtrace in Chicago and a renowned **microscopist** who had worked on major cases, including the murder of JonBenet Ramsey in Boulder, Colorado (*see* Chapter 4, page 56), and the Oklahoma City bombing.

Palenik examined the seven types of fiber found with the body and concluded immediately that they were from a cheap carpet made of odd pieces cast aside by major producers. He could link all of them to samples taken from Brown's house because the sloppy

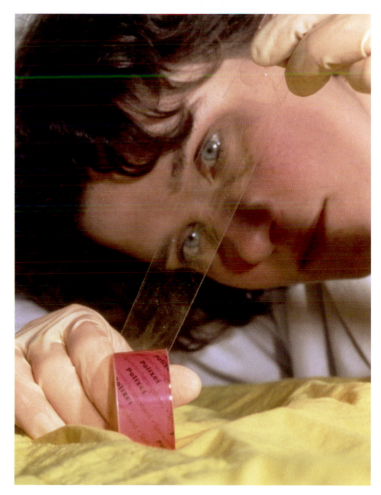

Forensic investigators commonly use tape for collecting fibers. Other methods include the use of tweezers or a vacuum.

construction made them unique. The pieces had the same combination of dyes, and some had bleached areas where the dye had not taken.

Alaskan state trooper, Sergeant Dallas Massie, said: "Skip told us you couldn't reproduce this carpet if you tried." The result was a murder conviction for Brown in 1998. This was overturned on a technicality, but Palenik returned to testify at the second trial, when Brown was, once again, found guilty.

The Amazing Case of Dr. Jeffrey MacDonald

One of the most notorious murders in U.S. history occurred in 1970. Not until 2006 were DNA tests being applied to fibers and hairs in an effort to free the convicted man, Dr. Jeffrey MacDonald. He had a successful career, attending Princeton University and Northwestern Medical School, before going on to become an Army doctor and a captain in the elite Green Berets. On February 17, 1970, however, his world came crashing down in his home at Fort Bragg in Fayetteville, North Carolina, and began one of America's most mysterious murder cases.

Army MPs (military police) found MacDonald's family dead: his wife, Colette, who was pregnant, and two young children, Kimberley, age five, and Kristin, age two. MacDonald himself had been stabbed in the chest with an ice pick and lay unconscious next to his wife.

Once revived, he said four hippies, including a blonde woman wearing a floppy hat, broke into his home. However, Bill Ivory, the U.S. Army's criminal investigator in charge of the crime scene, said the scenario MacDonald described "could not possibly have happened in that house." The scene was too perfectly laid out, even with a kitchen knife that was not the murder weapon lying next to Colette's body. Though fibers were found throughout the house, there were no pajama fibers in the living room, where MacDonald claimed his top had been torn while fighting off the intruders.

A military hearing, however, decided there was not enough evidence for a court martial, and MacDonald received an honorable discharge. He then hurt his cause by appearing to be comfortably relaxed on a popular talk show and the news program *60 Minutes*. In 1975, the federal government arrested MacDonald. He was tried in 1979 and the jury, who visited the crime scene, which remained untouched since the murders, declared him innocent.

Dr. Jeffrey MacDonald, accused in the murders of his pregnant wife and two young daughters, protested his innocence, citing inconclusive DNA tests on hair evidence.

As years went by, the case took another strange turn. For the first time, evidence was found in the government's files that had not previously been released: a black wool fiber wrapped around the murder weapon, a 22-inch (59-centimeter) blonde wig found at the scene, hairs found under Kristen's fingernail, and one hair in each of Colette's palms.

Next, Helena Stoeckly, the daughter of a retired Fort Bragg colonel, came forward to say she thought she had been with friends that night, taking drugs, and that she had worn a blonde wig under a floppy hat. The courts did not believe her, and the government decided the few hairs and fibers were not enough to merit a new trial. Stoeckly died in 1983 at the age of thirty-two.

Still, MacDonald was able to get DNA testing for the hairs and some blood evidence found in his house. On March 10, 2006, the results revealed that the hair under the fingernail of Kristen could not be identified, the hair on Colette's open palm did match MacDonald, and the one hair in her other palm was her own. Other hairs, however, could not be identified. No judgment based on these findings has yet been written, but MacDonald is launching his fourth appeal against his conviction. MacDonald now has a second wife, Kathryn. They married in 2002.

Notorious Killer

Fibers and hairs also helped convict one of the worst serial killers in U.S. history. The gruesome murders of twenty to thirty prostitutes began in late 1974 in the Riverside area of southern California. The police seemed helpless despite spending more than $100,000 on the elusive killer by 1991 and having twenty agencies being involved in the manhunt. Two days before Christmas, however, police stopped a white van whose driver, William Suff, had a suspended license and a lapsed vehicle registration. He had worked as a stock clerk for the county

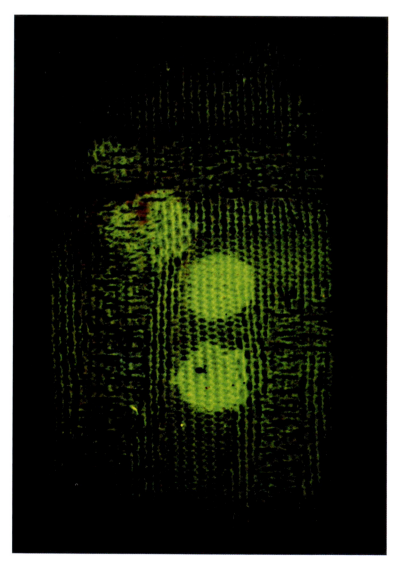

government. Checks revealed that he had served ten years in a Texas prison for beating his two-month-old daughter to death.

Still, the California court case against Suff in 1995 was circumstantial until forensic scientist Faye Springer, the state's foremost expert on hairs and fibers, linked microscopic samples of both hairs and fibers at two of the crime scenes to Suff. Fibers from his pillow, blanket, and the sleeping bag in his van

Ultraviolet scanning techniques can be used to show up trace evidence on material. Here, the technique shows up stained latent fingerprints on clothing fibers from a crime scene.

closely matched those found near the bodies of two victims. The van's carpet fibers were also found on a sock and T-shirt left on one body. Other fibers matched those found on his car seat. The jury found Suff guilty of multiple murders and recommended the death penalty, which he received.

Cotton fibers can be identified by their similarity to twisted ribbons. Cotton is seldom used as evidence, however, because it is so common.

Red Cloth

One of America's largest manhunts came about mainly because of some strips of red cloth. On October 1, 1993, in Petaluma, California, just north of San Francisco, twelve-year-old Polly Klaas had two friends staying for a sleepover party. As the girls and Polly's mother slept, a man entered the home, tied and gagged the three girls, and took Polly. This led to some 4,000 people searching for the girl over the next two months, and the FBI assigning twenty-four agents to work with the local police department.

There were no clues to Polly's whereabouts, or her abductor's, until a woman living in the Sonoma Valley area found strips of red cloth and some duct tape. This discovery concentrated the search. The FBI ran forensic tests and found that the cloth strips matched a pair of red dance tights the intruder had used to bind the other two girls. Investigators had, in the meantime, matched a palm print in the bedroom with Richard Davis, who was arrested as the massive hunt continued.

On December 4, the searchers in the field numbered 271, including dogs, horses, and dive teams, while crews totaling more than forty flew over the area.

The Department of Defense provided radar that could penetrate and picture objects buried up to 12 feet (4 meters) deep. The FBI kept fifteen evidence technicians ready to recover and examine any new evidence. This effort and the evidence overwhelmed the suspect, who confessed and led authorities to Polly's body. He had buried her alive. Davis was convicted in 1996 and sentenced to death.

CASE STUDY DRU'S LAW

In 2006, the discovery of multiple fibers helped lead to the conviction of the murderer of Dru Kathrina Sjodin, and to subsequent legislation called Dru's Law, which was passed that year and signed into law by President George W. Bush to set up a national sex-offender registry.

Sjodin, a student at the University of North Dakota, was kidnapped on November 22, 2003, from the Columbia Mall in Grand Forks, and later sexually assaulted and murdered. A registered sex offender Alfonso Rodriguez, Jr., age fifty, was arrested in connection with her disappearance. A knife in his car had blood that matched Sjodin's DNA. Her body was found on April 17, 2004, near Crookston, Minnesota when the snow melted.

In addition to the knife, a forensic scientist testified at the trial that black and pink fibers found in Rodriguez's car matched those from the black wool coat and pink cotton blouse Sjodin had been wearing. Other fiber links were found in the suspect's house, on Sjodin's clothing, and on a knife sheath near her car. A hair plucked from the black coat on the victim's body also matched Rodriguez's hair based on mitochondrial DNA (mtDNA) (*see* Chapter 2, page 33).

The FBI forensic scientist Les McCurdy testified that less than one-half of 1 percent of the Hispanic population had the same mtDNA as Rodriguez. The jury returned a guilty verdict and, although the death penalty would not have been possible in North Dakota, Rodriguez received it because he had crossed state lines.

Forensic work on the case of Sarah Payne (pictured), murdered in 2000 in England, led to the conviction of Roy Whiting despite the defense's efforts to downplay fiber tests.

Damning Evidence

Fibers linked to another man could not stop the execution in California in 1998 of Thomas Thompson, who lost a second appeal against his conviction for the 1981 assault and murder of twenty-year-old Ginger Fleischli in Laguna Beach. Even the U.S. Supreme Court had turned down the appeal. Police found Fleischli's buried body three days after she disappeared from an apartment 10 miles (16 kilometers) away, which Thompson shared with David Leich, the victim's ex-boyfriend. Fleischli had been stabbed five times in the right side of her head, which was wrapped with duct tape, a sheet, two towels, and her jacket. Her body was wrapped in a blanket, a sleeping bag, and rope.

Investigators found that fibers from the blanket matched fibers in Leitch's truck, and that the rope was smeared with paint from the car's trunk. Additional fibers were identical to the carpet in the apartment, which was stained with Fleischli's blood. DNA tests proved that Thompson had had sex with Fleischli. He and Leich fled to Mexico, though Leich later returned. Thompson stayed in Mexico, where he was arrested. He mentioned the girl being stabbed in the head, although the police had not released this information.

On November 4, 1983, Thompson was convicted of forcible rape and first-degree murder and sentenced to death. In 1997, he earned a stay of execution just hours before he was set to die, but died the next year by lethal injection in San Quentin state prison near San Francisco. He was the last death row inmate who could not choose the manner of his execution—the other option, soon to be introduced, was the gas chamber. Leich was convicted of second-degree murder for helping bury the body, and he received a sentence of fifteen years to life.

A Shoe and a Sweatshirt

Although the defense team in a court case usually has difficulty disputing forensic findings, lawyers have still argued against the importance of fiber evidence. In 2000, in England, Roy Whiting was accused of killing eight-year-old Sarah Payne in Kingston Gorse, Sussex. The girl's brother had seen a white van in the area, which police seized. In it, they found one of Sarah's shoes with a Velcro strap, which had trapped 350 fibers. Using a low-power microscope, investigators picked off the fibers with forceps. Four were red fibers that matched a sweatshirt found in the van owned by Roy Whiting. Others had been found in Sarah's hair and yet more in the bag she had been buried in—which matched the sweatshirt and a pair of Whiting's socks.

Despite this evidence, the defense team argued that there were too few fibers, and that these were not important because fiber tests are not as exact as DNA tests. Whiting was nevertheless found guilty in 2001 and sentenced to life imprisonment.

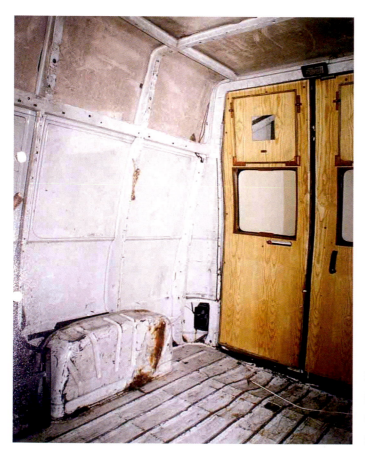

Identifying the Correct Source

Another common tactic defense teams use to downplay fiber evidence is to argue that the fibers came from other sources. This was the defense mounted when fibers linked David Westerfield to the 2002 kidnapping and

Hundreds of fibers were recovered from the white Fiat van of Roy Whiting, who murdered Sarah Payne. The forensic work took 17 months.

EDWARD OSCAR HEINRICH

The foundation for forensic science in the United States owes much to the chemist Edward Oscar Heinrich, who was known as America's Sherlock Holmes. During his career, Heinrich was credited with solving at least 2,000 cases. "Just the mention of his name was enough authority to send shudders through opposing counsel," noted Colin Evans in his 1996 book, *The Casebook of Forensic Detection*.

Heinrich was born in 1881 and, without a high school diploma, entered the University of California, Berkeley, where he received a degree in chemistry. After serving as the chief of police in Alameda, he returned to the university to begin his laboratory work investigating trace evidence. His success earned him the nickname of "the wizard of Berkeley" and led to national fame.

Heinrich indeed had Holmesian insight. He once declared that "a baker of cakes" had penned a ransom note, and the following investigations proved this to be true. In another case, when train robbers wore burlap sacks on their shoes to mask their scent from dogs, Heinrich simply traced the evidence to a local mechanic. His distinguished career continued until his death in 1953.

murder of seven-year-old Danielle Van Dam in San Diego, California. When police criminalist Jennifer Shen saw acrylic fibers in Westerfield's home, she recalled: "The long bright orange fibers were significant to me because I had seen a bright orange fiber somewhere else and that tagged my memory." She remembered a long orange fiber discovered on the victim "tangled in hair that was tangled around the necklace." The defense's response was to claim that it could have been blown by the wind onto the girl's decomposing body. They also suggested that it could have been transferred from the suspect to the girl's mother when they danced closely together, and then transferred to the girl—all on the night she disappeared. Neither suggestion swayed the jury, who convicted Westerfield. He received the death sentence in 2003.

chapter 6

Advances in Trace Evidence

DNA testing and more powerful laboratory instruments have led to huge advances in the use of trace evidence in forensic investigation.

Forensic medicine, also known as "legal medicine" and "medical jurisprudence," began to develop in Europe in the sixteenth century. Medicine had long been used to solve crimes in China, where coroners used a textbook first printed in 1248, *Hsi Duan Yu* (The Washing Away of Wrong). By 1598, an Italian doctor, Fortunatus Fidelis, began to practice modern forensic medicine as the "application of medical knowledge to legal questions." In the next century, medical witnesses were taking part in legal proceedings.

Another Italian physician, Paolo Zacchia, is considered to be one of the fathers of forensic medicine, and his nine-volume *Quaestiones Medico-Legales* (Medico-legal Questions), published between 1621 and 1651, gave legal medicine its name. By the eighteenth century, members of the public were well aware of eminent **toxicologists**, forensic pathologists, **autopsists**, and medical professors.

◁ **Taken in the 1940s, this photograph shows an expert examining a piece of fabric at the FBI laboratory in Washington, D.C. Today, the lab conducts more than one million tests each year.**

Progress in identifying trace evidence such as hairs and fibers has depended upon the development of microscopes with ever-greater magnification. In 1590, the Dutch spectacle maker Zacharias Janssen and his father, Hans Janssen, used a tube with lenses at each end to design the first practical microscope with a magnification range of three times to nine times. In 1670, a Dutch amateur scientist, Anton van Leeuwenhoek, developed the first precision microscope in order to inspect cloth fibers (*see opposite page*). Using a single lens, he increased the magnification up to 270 times.

Enter the Microscope

In the meantime, the compound microscope was being refined in Germany. Johannes Kepler had suggested using **convex lenses** for the eyepiece and **objective**, and Christoph Scheiner constructed a microscope of this type in around 1628, which provided a larger field of view and served as the prototype for modern microscopes. About 1684, the Dutch physicist Christiaan Huygens devised an effective two-lens eyepiece.

However, microscopes did not make an impact on criminal investigations until after William Nichol

An early microscope designed by England's Robert Hooke, who contributed to many scientific fields. His observations were published in 1665 in his book *Micrographia*.

PROFILE ANTON VAN LEEUWENHOEK

Often called "the father of microscopy," Anton van Leeuwenhoek was born in 1632 in Delft, Holland. He worked as an apprentice in a dry goods store, counting the threads in cloth. To do this work, he had to use a primitive magnifying glass, so he became determined to develop a more powerful instrument. After teaching himself how to grind and polish lenses, Leeuwenhoek devised new methods to create a greater curvature to produce the finest magnification of his time—up to 270 times. He went on to create exquisite gold and silver instruments with a single lens of very short focus, which gave a better result than the compound microscopes then in use.

Leeuwenhoek soon forgot about counting threads, and developed a new obsession—biology. In 1674, he was the first to discover bacteria and give an accurate description of red blood corpuscles (living cells). His research included the structure of muscle and teeth, and led to descriptions of the life cycle of the weevil, flea, ant, eel, and mussel. His work was published by the Royal Society of England, which also made him a member in 1680. He died in 1723.

invented the polarizing light microscope in 1828. The French forensic scientist Henry-Louis Bayard first noted, in 1836, the different microscopic characteristics of various fabrics. By 1898, Paul Jesrich, a forensic chemist in Berlin, began to take photomicrographs (photographs taken through microscopes) in order to compare two bullets.

Trace Evidence and Photography

Trace evidence was officially recorded for the first time in 1786 in Lancaster, England, and helped convict John Toms for the murder of Edward Culshaw. Investigators found in Culshaw's head a wad made of crushed paper used to keep the powder and balls in the muzzles of pistols. The wad was a piece of

The German pathologist Rudolph Virchow was the first person to study hair as evidence. He also developed a standard of autopsy still used today.

torn newspaper, and the torn edge matched another piece found in Toms' pocket. In 1816, in Warwick, England, a trace impression led to the murderer of a young maidservant who had been drowned in a shallow pool, and whose body bore marks of violence. In addition to footprints and scattered grains of wheat and chaff, police discovered in the damp ground near the pool an impression from corduroy cloth with a sewn patch. They examined the patched corduroy breeches of a farm laborer who had been threshing wheat, and found a perfect match with the impression on the earth. Then in 1835, Scotland Yard's Henry Goddard was able to trace a bullet found at a crime scene by matching a visible flaw on its surface to the mold that produced it.

In the 1860s, investigators were beginning to use photography to document crime scenes. Near the turn of the century, R.A. Reiss, a professor at the University of Lausanne, Switzerland, established a forensic photography department, and in 1903 this became part of the Lausanne Institute of Police Science.

In 1879, the German pathologist Rudolph Virchow was the first to study hair as evidence, but he warned about its limitations in court cases. Arthur Conan Doyle gave trace evidence popular treatment in the first Sherlock Holmes story, which was published in 1887. Toward the end of the nineteenth century, it figured in more and more criminal investigations. In 1891, Hans Gross, a professor of criminal law at the University of Graz in Austria, published *Criminal Investigation*, the first comprehensive volume on using physical evidence to solve crimes.

The Exchange Principle

In 1904, Georg Popp, a forensic scientist in Frankfurt, Germany, demonstrated the exchange principle (*see* page 85) in the case of the strangulation death of Eva Disch, a seamstress who was murdered with her own scarf in a bean field. The evidence was a handkerchief with nasal mucus that contained traces of coal, snuff, and grains of minerals, including **hornblend**. The police had a suspect, Karl Laubach, who worked in a coal-burning gasworks and also part-time in a gravel pit. Popp examined Laubach's fingernails and found coal and the mineral grains, mostly hornblend. Laubach also used snuff.

Popp's detailed search included two layers of dirt in the suspect's pant cuffs.

The lower layer matched the soil at the crime scene, and the layer covering it matched soil on the path Laubach had taken home. When presented with this evidence, Laubach confessed. This was the first time geologic, or earthen, evidence had been used in a criminal case, though it had been predicted in the Sherlock Holmes books. A Frankfurt newspaper reported the story under the headline "The Microscope as Detective."

The first comprehensive study of hair, *Le poil de l'homme et des animaux* (Human and Animal Hair), was published in 1910 by Victor Balthazard, professor of forensic medicine at the Sorbonne in Paris, with Marcelle Lambert. This was also the year that hair strands from Rosella Rousseau were found at the scene of Germaine Bichon's murder and resulted in her confession (*see* Chapter 3, page 37).

Advances in Police Procedure

The collection of trace evidence was becoming more sophisticated in the early years of the twentieth century. In 1916, Albert Schneider of Berkeley, California, became the first person to use a vacuum device to collect crime-scene evidence. That same year at Berkeley, the chief of police, August Vollmer, established the School of Criminology at the University of California, Berkeley. He went on, in 1923, to begin the first forensic laboratory in the United States, in the Los Angeles Police Department. A year later, the United States Bureau of Investigation, which later became the Federal Bureau of Investigation (FBI), set up an Identification Division and established its fingerprint file. In 1929, the first private forensic laboratory began operating just north of Chicago.

The latter came about because of the expertise of a cardiologist, Dr. Calvin Goddard, who in 1925 with Philip Gravelle had invented the comparison microscope. Two years later, he used it to match bullet casings and uphold the convictions of Nicola Sacco and Bartolomeo Vanzetti for two murders.

In 1929, Goddard's investigation of the infamous St. Valentine's Day Massacre case resulted in the establishment of a new crime laboratory. On February 14, 1929, members of Al "Scarface" Capone's gang, dressed as policemen, gunned down seven members of rival gangster George "Bugs" Moran's gang in a Chicago warehouse. The crime-scene investigators recovered seventy shell casings, which Goddard identified as coming from Thompson submachine guns.

EVERY CONTACT LEAVES A TRACE

In 1904, the French forensic scientist Edmond Locard first put forward the forensic idea that "every contact leaves a trace" in his *L'enquete criminelle et les methodes scientifique* (Criminal Enquiry and Scientific Methods). Locard also directed the first true crime laboratory, in Lyon, France, and his idea about trace evidence is now known as the Locard exchange principle. He presented a colorful description of how a criminal is caught by trace evidence:

"Wherever he steps, whatever he touches, whatever he leaves, even unconsciously, will serve as a silent witness against him. Not only his fingerprints or his footprints, but his hair, the fibers from his clothes, the glass he breaks, the tool mark he leaves, the paint he scratches, the blood or body fluid he deposits or collects. All of these, and more, bear mute witness against him. This is evidence that does not forget. It is not confused by the excitement of the moment. It is not absent because human witnesses are. It is factual evidence. Physical evidence cannot be wrong, it cannot perjure itself, it cannot be wholly absent. Only human failure to find it, study, and understand it, can diminish its value."

Edmond Locard was known as "the Sherlock Holmes of France." He established his crime laboratory in 1910, and worked until his death in 1966.

85

The perpetrators of the 1929 St. Valentine's Day Massacre in Chicago were caught by using the comparison microscope invented by Dr. Calvin Goddard and Philip Gravelle.

He then used the new comparison microscope to compare the bullet casings from the murder scene with those from the police's Thompsons, and found that the casings did not match. This discovery meant that no real police had been involved. The police then raided the home of a Capone hit man and found two Thompsons. They later proved that these guns had been used in the murders.

Impressed by Goddard's expertise in the case, two businessmen on the coroner's inquest jury funded the Scientific Crime Detection Laboratory on the campus of Northwestern University in Evanston, Illinois. It provided experts with the tools and technology they needed to investigate trace evidence, analyze blood, and compare firearms and fingerprints.

To see much smaller details on trace evidence, forensic scientists needed a microscope that could actually bypass light and use a different type of "illumination." This came in 1931, when the German scientists Ernst Ruska and Max Knott invented the electron microscope, which speeded up electrons in a vacuum to make their wavelength only one-hundred-thousandth the measure of that of white light. Investigators could now view objects as small as the diameter of an atom.

DNA Testing

The development of DNA testing in the 1980s allowed investigators to match more hairs with grater accuracy and resulted in more convictions. A more powerful refinement in the twenty-first century is the DNA Low Copy Number method (DNA LCN), which was developed in the laboratories of Britain's Forensic Science Service. Relying on a technique known as polymerase chain reaction (PCR) amplification (*see* Chapter 2, page 29), DNA LCN can obtain DNA profiles from samples containing only a few cells of a single hair—ten times less than normal DNA testing. However, this increases the analysis time, which usually takes several weeks, and the high sensitivity of DNA LCN requires forensic scientists to run the tests and analyze the results very carefully, since other DNA unconnected with the offense may be detected.

The technique has already led to highly publicized convictions. In Australia in 2005, Bradley Murdoch was jailed for life for the murder of British tourist Peter Falconio in 2001 on a remote stretch of road. Plastic cable used to bind the hands of Falconio's girlfriend, Joanne Lees, was recovered at the scene. DNA LCN tests on samples of the cable reveal a link to Murdoch's DNA.

Recently, DNA tests have led to many prisoners being proven innocent, which has resulted in calls to retain samples for decades instead of days. A Canadian case proved this point. In Manitoba, in 2004, a review committee wanted to test the DNA of hair used to convict Kyle Unger and Timothy Houlahan for the 1990 killing of sixteen-year-old Brigitte Grenier. The single strand of hair evidence had been destroyed as a matter of police policy, which required such evidence to be kept for only thirty days after all appeals had been exhausted. The Royal Canadian Mounted Police are now working on new guidelines for preserving evidence, with a recommendation that it be retained for twenty years in murder cases.

New Tools, New Methods

Changes are on the horizon in the manner of detecting and analyzing hairs and fibers as new forensic instruments are introduced. The shift is toward portable analytical equipment known as the "lab on a microchip." The near future will usher in miniaturization and automation. "I think we can see analysis being performed faster and in the field by qualified analysts," said forensic scientist Keith Inman. "We should be moving to the day when investigative leads can be provided to the detective in the field, rather than months later in the lab." Others anticipate the immediate availability of all types of evidence on databases, and some even transmitted by satellites.

As well as taking specialized analytical instruments to the crime scene, investigators will depend more upon automated finding and analysis systems. The Maxcan fiber finder, for example, is a new device that has proven to be as effective in locating fibers as a manual search. Automated analysis will also make a difference in the courtroom. According to Dr. Brian D. Andresen of Andresen Forensics Sciences at Livermore, California, these new systems will appeal to prosecutors because there is no bias in the interpretation of the data. "Defense lawyers," he adds, "will not be fond of analysis automation because there will be no witness to cross-examine."

The immediate future will also see more professional workshops, conferences, and training to develop a standard approach to hair and fabric

TOOLS **SEM**

The powerful scanning electronic microscope (SEM) is the only instrument that produces images of ultramicroscopic objects in a detailed and realistic three-dimensional form. A sample of forensic evidence is placed inside the SEM's vacuum column, which has an airtight door. Air is pumped out and an **electron** gun at the top sends out a fine beam of electrons that magnetic lenses control and focus to a point. Scanning coils move the beam back and forth over the sample. The impact of the beam knocks electrons from the surface of the sample. Another device then counts these electrons and sends them to an amplifier so that the image is displayed on a viewing monitor. The image is in black and white, but color can be applied artificially if desired.

A technician uses a 250,000 power electron microscope in 1971 at North American Rockwell's Automotive Technical Center in Troy, Michigan.

A hair and fiber examiner with the FBI laboratory examines the contents of an evidence container during a trial in 2005.

examination. The need to establish a sound foundation for future testing is now at the forefront of forensic science thinking. West Virginia University and the National Forensic Science Technology Center in Largo, Florida run workshops and produce reference materials and guidelines for examining human and animal hairs, as well as electronic reference materials to assist forensic scientists in the study of hair characteristics.

CASE STUDY | **HISTORICAL HAIR**

In 2003, the DNA testing of hair cut from the French Queen Marie-Antoinette when she was a child in the 1700s helped solve a historical mystery when it was compared with DNA from a child's heart.

After Louis XVI and Marie Antoinette were guillotined during the French revolution, the fate of their ten-year-old son was unknown. It was generally believed that the prince had died in prison, but many believed he had escaped and even produced heirs. Fortunately, a heart of a child in the prison had been preserved, but there was no proof that it was the prince's heart.

Historians arranged for DNA tests in the summer of 2003, which proved conclusively that the heart did belong to the prince, a result that dashed the hopes of any pretenders claiming direct descent from Louis XVI and Marie Antoinette.

Marie Antoinette, born in Austria, became unpopular in France because of her extravagance. She and Louis XVI were captured trying to escape the country.

Glossary

acetate a semi-transparent sheet made from cellulose acetate

alibi the defense by an accused person of having been elsewhere at the time an offense was committed

anagen phase the growth phase of hair, in which DNA is abundant

autopsists scientists who dissect and examine dead bodies to discover the cause of death

catagen phase the transitional growth period for hair

chloroform a colorless, volatile, heavy liquid used as a solvent and considered hazardous to the environment

convex lenses lenses that are curved or rounded like the exterior of a sphere

cortex the part of a hair that surrounds the central core; it contains the pigment that determines the hair's color

criminalist another name for a forensic scientist, especially one who investigates crime scenes

cuticle the outside sheath of a hair; it has overlapping scales

DNA deoxyribonucleic acid, which is any of various nucleic acids that are the basis of heredity; they are constructed of a double helix held together by hydrogen bonds

false-positive an incorrect positive result from a forensic test, such as contaminated evidence being linked to the wrong suspect

forensic science profession that collects and investigates physical evidence from a crime scene and analyzes it with scientific tests to apprehend the criminal

homicide murder

hornblend a complex mixture of minerals found in rocks such as granite

laudanum a preparation of opium (a narcotic drug consisting of the dried juice of the opium poppy)

light microscopy also known as optical microscopy—a technique that involves passing visible light transmitted through or reflected from an object through a single lens

medulla the central core of a hair

melanin pigment on the skin and hair, with special properties for binding traces of drugs to hairs

microscopist someone who is expert in using a microscope

mitochondrial DNA (mtDNA) a form of DNA found in tiny mitochondria cell structures; it is inherited maternally, so is the best source for determining family relationships

morphology the essential form and structure of something

neutron activation analysis technique to identify elements, as in a hair, by placing a sample in the core of a nuclear reactor and bombarding it with neutrons to produce measurable gamma radiation

nucleus the subcellular part of a cell that contains the cell's chromosomes (basic units of DNA)

objective the primary optical element in a microscope (also in a telescope or camera)

organic polymers molecules consisting of many identical parts that are chemically bonded

pathologists scientists who study the causes and treatment of diseases

petrochemicals any of a large number of chemicals made from petroleum (gasoline) or natural gas

phenol also known as carbolic acid—a colorless, corrosive, poisonous, crystalline solid, with a sweet odor; found in coal tar and wood tar

phosphorus a chemical element that is an essential for all living cells, and is found in DNA (deoxyribonucleic acid) and RNA (ribonucleic acid)

polymerase chain reaction (PCR) a technique that uses the enzyme polymerase to copy and multiply DNA by millions of times to provide a sample large enough to be analyzed

sulfur radiation energy emitted from the non-metallic element sulfur, which occurs singly or combined, especially in sulfides (any of a number of organic compounds with a sulfur atom attached to two carbon atoms) or sulfates (a salt or ester of sulfuric acid)

telogen phase a resting phase in the growth of hair, in which hairs are routinely shed

toxicologists scientists who examine the effects of poisonous substances

trace evidence physical evidence left at a crime scene, such as hairs, fibers, body fluid, and blood

viscose a golden brown solution made by treating cellulose with caustic alkali solution and carbon disulfide, and used in the manufacture of the smooth textile rayon

Learn More About

Numerous sources are available for further research into procedures and cases involving hair and fibers, as well as other trace elements and the general topic of forensic science. Below are suggested books and Web sites that link to government bureaus, professional bodies, magazine and newspaper articles, official reports, and other sources.

Books

Ackerman, Thomas. *FBI Careers*. Indianapolis, Indiana: Jist Works, 2005.

Camenson, Blythe. *Opportunities in Forensic Science Careers*. New York: McGraw-Hill Publishing, 2001.

Evans, Colin. *The Casebook of Forensic Detection: How Science Solved 100 of the World's Most Baffling Crimes*. New York: Wiley Publishing, 1998.

Federal Bureau of Investigation. *Handbook of Forensic Science*. Toronto, Canada: Books for Business, 2001.

Fisher, Barry. *Techniques in Crime Scene Investigation*. Boca Raton, Florida: CRC Press, 2003.

Fisher, Barry, David Fisher and Jason Kolowski. *Forensics Demystified*. New York: McGraw-Hill Publishing, 2006.

Fletcher, Connie. *Every Contact Leaves a Trace: Crime Scene Experts Talk About Their Work from Discovery Through Verdict*. New York: St. Martin's Press, 2006.

Funkhluser, John. *Forensic Science for High School Students*. Dubuque, Iowa: Kendall Hunt Publishing Company, 2005.

Houck, Max M. *Trace Evidence*. New York: Facts on File, 2006.

Lee, Henry C. and Howard A. Harris. *Physical Evidence in Forensic Science*. Tucson, Arizona: Lawyers & Judges Publishing Company, 2000.

Owen, David. *Hidden Evidence: Forty True Crimes and How Forensic Science Helped Solve Them*. Ontario, Canada: Firefly Books, 2000.

Saferstein, Richard. *Criminalistics: An Introduction to Foresic Science*. New Jersey: Prentice Hall, 2003.

White, Jonathan R. *Terrorism and Homeland Security*. Belmont, California: Wadsworth Publishing, 2005.

Web Sites

Bureau of Alcohol, Tobacco, Firearms and Explosives: www.atf.gov

CIA for kids:www.cia.gov/cia/ciakids/govagency .shtml

FBI for kids: www.fbi.gov/fbikids.htm

FBI laboratory: www.fbi.gov/hq/lab/labhome.htm

Fiber and Fabric: http://42explore.com/fibers.htm

Introduction to Forensic Fiber Examination: www.fbi.gov/hq/lab/fsc/backissu/april1999/houckch1.htm

Metropolitan Police Forensic Services: www.met.police.uk/scd/units/forensic_services. htm

Police Technology and Forensic Science: http://inventors.about.com/od/fstartinventions/a/forensic.htm

Royal Canadian Mounted Police: www.rcmp-grc.gc.ca

Trace Evidence: Hair: www.crimeandclues.com/hair_evidence.htm

Transportation Security Administration (TSA): www.tsa.gov

About the Author

John D. Wright is an American author and editor living in England. He has been a reporter for *Time* and *People* magazines, covering such subjects as politics, crime, and social welfare. He has also worked as a journalist for the U.S. Navy and for newspapers in Alabama and Tennessee. In 2002, he contributed to the *Crime and Detection* series for Mason Crest Publishers. He holds a Ph.D. degree in Communications from the University of Texas and has taught journalism in three universities.

Quoted Sources

p. 15—*Bioscience Explained*, Vol. 2, No. 1, by Robert Kronstrand

p. 17—Dr. Fred Smith, UAB Publications; Spring, 2004

p. 22—Dr. Henry C. Lee: www.crimelibrary.com/criminal_mind/forsensics/lee/1.html

pp. 25 and 27—Dr. Henry C. Lee: www.crimelibrary.com/criminal_mind/forensics/lee/2.html

p. 38—Dick Bisbing, *Dallas Morning News*, March 31, 2002

p. 38—Charles Linch, *Dallas Morning News*, March 31, 2002

p. 39—Ben Weider, *The Guardian*; May 5, 2000

p. 40—Steve Mills and Ken Armstrong, *Chicago Tribune*, November 18, 1999

p. 42—Johnny Cochran: www.courttv.com/trials/ojsimpson/weekly/21.html

p. 47—Ronald M. Huber, *The Cavalier Daily*, September 26, 2000

p. 51—Larry Craig, *The Washington Times*, December 19, 2001

pp. 53 and 55—Douglas Deedrick, *Forensic Science Communications*, July 2000

p. 61—Douglas Deedrick, *Forensic Science Communications*, July 2000

p. 63—Alec Jeffreys: The Royal Society at www.royalsoc.ac.uk/page.asp?id=1523

p. 70—Dallas Massie, *Popular Science*, September 2002

p. 70—CBS News: www.cbs.com/stories/2005/11/02/48hours/main1002954.shtml

p. 77—Jennifer Shen: www.courttv.com/trials/westerfield/062502_ctv.html

p. 85—*Crime Investigation*, by Edmond Locard (trans. Paul Kirk), Interscience Publishing, 1953

p. 88—Keith Inman: www.courttv.com/talk/chat_transcripts/rudin-inman.html

p. 88—Brian D. Andresen: Andresen Forensic Sciences at www.designthink.com/afs/faq.php

Index

Page numbers in *italics* refer to photographs.